GROWING UP SCARED?

The Psychological Effect of the Nuclear Threat on Children

Benina Berger Gould, Susan Moon, Judith Van Hoorn,
editors

Open Books
Berkeley, California

Copyright (c) 1986 by Benina Berger Gould, Susan Moon
and Judith Van Hoorn
ISBN: 0-931416-04-3

Cover design by Susan Moon
Photographs by Pamela Weaver
Printed by Thomson-Shore, Dexter, Michigan

OPEN BOOKS
1631 Grant Street
Berkeley, California

GROWING UP SCARED? can be ordered from:
The Nuclear Ecology Research Project
P.O. Box 9998
Berkeley, CA 94709
$10.00 per book + $1.00 postage for first book,
+ 50¢ each additional copy.

TABLE OF CONTENTS

ACKNOWLEDGEMENTS   1

INTRODUCTION   3
    Benina Berger Gould, L.C.S.W.

FOREWORD: PUBLIC HEALTH AND THE NUCLEAR THREAT   7
    Joyce Lashof, M.D.

Three Persectives

PROVIDING A CONTEXT FOR PEACE EDUCATION   13
    Ron Lally, Ed.D.

APPROACHING THE NUCLEAR THREAT IN CLINICAL WORK   25
WITH CHILDREN AND THEIR FAMILIES
    John E. Mack, M.D.

THE POLITICAL PSYCHOLOGY OF DETERRENCE   39
    Richard Smoke, Ph.D.

Reports on Research Findings

EXPLORING YOUTH'S REACTION TO THE THREAT   49
OF NUCLEAR WAR
    Jeffrey Gould, M.D.

FACING THE NUCLEAR THREAT: 57
COMPARISONS OF ADOLESCENTS AND ADULTS
    Judith Van Hoorn, Ph.D.

ADOLESCENCE AND THE NUCLEAR THREAT IN FINLAND: 77
ANXIETY AND OPTIMISM
    Tytti Solantaus, M.D.

Young People and Social Action

YOUTH EMPOWERMENT FORUM: 93
A PANEL DISCUSSION WITH ELEVEN YOUNG PEOPLE
 Benina Berger Gould, L.C.S.W., moderator

YOUTH ACTIVISM AND EMPOWERMENT 119
 Laurie Olsen, M.A.T.

ADVOCACY WITH TEENAGERS FACING 135
THE NUCLEAR THREAT
 Eve Eden, M.S.W.

EDUCATION OR EXHORTATION? POSTMORTEM 141
OF A "BAD" VIDEOTAPE
 Alan Marcus and Lotte Marcus, Ph.D.

Workshop Summaries

THE NUCLEAR THREAT IN THE CLINICAL HOUR 153
 Ellen Becker, M.F.C.C.,
 and Barbara Green, L.C.S.W.

COMMUNITY MENTAL HEALTH AND THE NUCLEAR THREAT 159
 Howard Hamburger, M.F.C.C.,
 and Deborah Weinstein, M.F.C.C.

AFFECTING PUBLIC POLICY 169
 Eve Eden, M.S.W.,
 and Wendy Roberts, M.S.W.

CONCLUSION: WHERE DO WE GO FROM HERE? 175
 Susan Moon

Appendix: A Review of the Literature

CHILDREN, ADOLESCENTS AND THE THREAT　　　　183
OF NUCLEAR WAR: AN INTERNATIONAL PERSPECTIVE
    Monika Eisenbud, M.D., Judith Van Hoorn, Ph.D.,
    and Benina Berger Gould, L.C.S.W.

NOTES ON CONTRIBUTORS　　　　219

ACKNOWLEDGEMENTS

Much sweat went into the compiling of this book. Each editor has her own support or affinity group to thank for the ability to survive over the long haul of our involvement as women in peace work. We worked as a team, responsibilities were shared, and decisions were made together.

In connection with the actual conference planning, I wish to thank Lloyd Churgin, of the University of California Extension School, who encouraged me to plan a conference that would fit my fantasy, and who urged me and helped me to go for it, one hundred percent. Barbara Green, Wendy Roberts, Howard Hamburger, Laurie Olsen, Deborah Weinstein, and Ellen Becker spent long and hard hours in the planning which was necessary to make the conference a reality.

I especially want to thank Jeff Gould, Eve Eden, Carol Oppenheimer, Sarah Rosenthal, Kathy Kostello, and Leslie Knutson, who pioneered the research with me that provided the basis for the conference, and who worked relentlessly, without money, to represent what our young people are thinking and feeling about living with the threat of nuclear war.

Without the help and encouragement of Richard Smoke, Barbara Hazard, Robert Blomberg, Norah Holmgren, and the Peace and Common Security Institute, this work would not have been transformed into a book. Their support has been generously given since the inception of the Nuclear Ecology Research Project.

Finally, I would like to thank the young people from all over the country who participated in the original research. Special thanks go to my children, Ezra and Alison, to Susan's children, Noah and Sandy, and to Judith's children, Alia and Peter, all of whom have contributed in their own ways to our joint struggle for a secure future.

We would also like to thank all of the following people, without whose help this book would not have seen the light of day: Donald Bloch, Richard Carlton, M.D., Richard Chasin, M.D., Brenda Engel, David and Faith Friedlander, Alice Hayes, Arlie Hochschild, Eva Lieberman, Jon Levine, M.D., Francois Leydet, Physicians for Social Responsibility - Berkeley, Physicians for Social Responsibility - Stanford, Ken Porter, Jackie Riskin, Ellen Rosenau, Anna Scheffey, Francie Shaw, D.W. Silby, Cornelia St. John, Nancy St. John, Naomi and Milton Taubman, Derek Van Hoorn, Leni von Blanckensee, Steven Zeitlin.

        Benina Berger Gould

INTRODUCTION

Benina Berger Gould

The conference on which this book is based was a very special conference, whose purpose was to address the issue of the psychological effect of the nuclear threat on children, and to consider strategies for action. We brought together a group of people from the four broad areas of political science, psychology, education, and public health, both to learn from each other and to work together in strategy planning groups. Conference participants included a panel of real "experts" - fourteen young people of varied racial and economic backgrounds, ranging in age from 12 to 18. The cross-fertilization of different disciplines and the multi-generational approach created an intense and stimulating atmosphere for the two days we all worked and learned together.

In addition to bringing our diverse community together, the conference provided us an opportunity to work on strategies that would move the issue from the research and knowledge area to that of public policy and social action. How does the fact that young people are being affected in a harmful manner become a concern of policy makers and people in power? A number of ideas were presented for addressing the problem on an individual, school, clinical, community and public policy level.

Now, a year later, I ask the question, "Was this a successful conference?" Needless to say, the interdisciplinary nature and richness of the presentations and dialogue deepened our understanding of the public health and psychological aspects of this problem, and enabled us to probe new options for responding. When I ask what, specifically, is the psychological effect, for children, of growing up under the nuclear shadow, I am not sure we have moved as far as we could have, but we have certainly learned a great deal. We know young people have a sense of despair and futurelessness, that they are not sure they will grow up. We can conjecture that living under this threat causes toxic stress on body and spirit, the extent of which may not be known for years to come. We are also learning that forums which provide a way for young people to participate in social change are empowering and inspiring to them.

Some see the nuclear threat as providing an unparalelled opportunity for growth and change. Others see a lack of affinity among people, a sense of alienation in a society addicted to militarism. Still others point to the connection between our defense buildup and the disempowerment of women. There are many theories, but we all would agree that to live with the possibility of all-out nuclear war is to live with a damaging fear. As one child states, "I think about war every day, not knowing what's going to happen to me when I'm walking to school."

The conference was an ambitious one. We asked each other then, and we continue to ask, what to do. What are our strategies for action? The major problem that continues to face us is how to bring into focus the mental health problem caused by the threat of nuclear war, so that our society addresses this problem as a priority.

In our continuing work for peace, we need now to look for interventions which can help young people, their parents, and their teachers to work together in an empowering way to bring about democratic social change. We are all in this race for survival together, and our children have spoken clearly of the horrors and fears they experience on a day-to-day basis. As a mother, family therapist, and researcher, I know children have many problems besides the nuclear threat to cope with as they grow up. I am proud to see adults and children come together as equals, and consider in these pages how to make the planet a safer place in which to grow.

Note: GROWING UP SCARED?, although based on the taped proceedings of the conference, is not a transcript, but a collection of written pieces. With the exception of the youth forum, which we have included verbatim as we heard it on the tape, all of the articles in this book have been edited or rewritten.

FOREWARD

Joyce Lashof, M.D.

The psychological effect of the nuclear threat is a public health issue, and one that should be addressed from a public health point of view. What do I mean by that? As a professor of Public Health, I like to try to define for our students the methodology a good public health professional uses in addressing a problem, and I'd like to apply that methodology here.

First of all, you have to define the problem, and here the problem is defined as that of the psychological impact of the threat of nuclear war on children. Having defined the problem, you want to determine what is the scope of that problem. What's the population at risk? Is it the same across age, class, social status? How do these factors influence the problem? Research on these very questions is described in the following pages.

Having decided what is the population at risk, you want to know how the problem really affects that population, not only in obvious ways, but in more subtle ways, for example in this case, from the extremes of depression to the more subtle effect on learning ability because of distraction. How does the problem affect children's daily lives? What impact does it have on what they do, on how they view their schools, their studies, their future? You want to understand the ramifications. Then you want to look at what factors are really important in bringing about this problem. Is this an imagined problem? Is it something that's just stirred up by the media, by rabble rousers? Or are there real reasons for this problem, and what is its scope?

How many of these factors pertain to the individual, and how many are societal issues? You want to look at those issues and examine them and understand them.

When you have defined the problem, decided its scope, looked at its ramifications, looked at the factors that are important, once you've done all that, then you come to the next step, which is to ask: what do we do about the problem? Where do we intervene? How do we intervene? Obviously, our best intervention is that which can eliminate the cause entirely and thus prevent the problem. That's the goal of public health. Identify, find the causes, eliminate the causes and eliminate the problem.

That's obviously not so easy in this case. I'm sure there is no one who wouldn't like to eliminate the problem of nuclear war with a wave of the hand. So the question is, then, how do you work at eliminating the problem, and what is gained by the effort? What impact does working on the problem have on the people involved? By that I mean, if you can't eliminate the problem, just like that, do you then teach young people to try to cope with the problem, do you try to get them to deny the problem, do you try to get them to ignore the problem? Do you just ignore the problem yourself because you don't think you can do anything about it, and maybe if you ignore it the child won't worry about it? Or do you really begin to engage children in finding solutions to the problem, to begin to be active and concerned and to feel that they can have an impact? One of the interesting lessons from social epidemiology is that morbidity and mortality seem to be very much related to how much control we have over our own lives. And I suspect that in this case the issue of control is going to be a major factor. If we feel we can make no impact and have no control, then we're not apt to have much effect. But if we can engage ourselves and our children in addressing the problem, and we begin to feel that we can take hold and can have an impact, that in itself will be a positive step.

These, I think, are the issues, that's what the conference was about, and that's what this book is about. To my knowledge this was the first conference in this country to deal with this specific issue, and to look at its ramifications and its solutions.

Three Perspectives

PROVIDING A CONTEXT FOR PEACE EDUCATION

Ron Lally, Ed.D.

　　I am a student of children and families. Since 1966 I have been involved in developing and evaluating programs designed to strengthen child and family functioning. Over the years I have seen far too many American children raised to adulthood with high levels of fear and anger, and with organizing views of life that project fellow humans as enemies. I have seen many young people who grow up doubting themselves and acting ashamed of who they are. It seems that, in the 1980's, violence, selfishness and lack of purpose are becoming increasingly common terms to describe more and more of our young.
　　I find these conditions troubling in the best of circumstances; but these descriptions of youth are particularly troublesome, given the world conditions in which these new adults will function. When the children now in our schools and daycare centers grow to adulthood they will be called upon by world conditions to interact with others on the most serious life and death survival issues that have ever existed. No other generation will have been asked to expand so widely their range of communication and collaboration, to be so inclusive in their visions, and to be so global in their solutions. American children need our help to raise them above their legacy of provincialism and short-sighted selfishness specifically because they will be called upon to alter the world view of generations to fit new facts of life.
　　Yet the way adult society currently deals with world issues of the most deadly nature leaves children with

little room for hope and few models to emulate. Some personality theorists call this situation a national crisis in character development. One of the most insightful observers of emotional development in children, a person who has been charting the impact of events on the developing character of the young since the early 1950's, Dr. Sybille Escalona of Yeshiva University of New York, describes her view of the impact of current adult behavior with regard to issues of peace and war on the character development of children. She states:

> Growing up in a social environment that tolerates and ignores the risk of total destruction by means of voluntary human action tends to foster those patterns of personality functioning that can lead to a sense of powerlessness and cynical resignation. By the same token the development of those characteristics that can generate and support future oriented collective social action are made more difficult to come by in the present social climate. In short, I believe that growing up in full knowledge of the fact that there may be no future, and that the adult world seems unable to combat the threat, can render the next generation less well equipped to avert actual catastrophe than they would be if the same threat existed in a different social climate...

Her message is frightening. Current adult functioning fosters in children attitudes of powerlessness and cynical resignation at the very time that the antitheses of these attitudes are needed.

The thesis of my talk today is that if peace education efforts are to truly aid these children they must be comprehensive in design and combat the development of feelings of hopelessness in young children. Peace education efforts must address not only the nuclear emergencies that confront us but must also address the less visible underpinnings of personality that govern motives and character in individuals. Current peace education efforts sometimes play down these issues of character because the nuclear emergency is so patently obvious and demanding of emergency attention. The nuclear context screams at educators to take action. Shouldn't children know that we live on a planet which contains fifty thousand nuclear warheads poised and ready to trigger species death? Shouldn't teachers make it obvious to children that the fundamental problems people face today and will face if they grow to maturity are global? Shouldn't they know, as Henry Steele Commager (1982) so vividly stated, that:

> Every major problem that confronts us is global -- energy, pollution, and the destruction of the oceans and seas, the erosion of agricultural and forest lands, the control of epidemics and of plant and animal diseases, famine in large parts of Asia and Africa, and population increase...inflation, international terrorism, nuclear pollution, and nuclear arms control...these problems require the cooperation of statesmen, scientists, and moral philosophers in every country. (p.22)

Shouldn't they learn that the operational logic of nation states no longer provides security to citizens and that war between nations with a nuclear capacity has become unwinnable? Yes, because although argument continues about these conclusions, the weight of scientific evidence becomes more and more convincing in support of them. The more that's learned about subjects such as the ramifications of a nuclear winter and pollutant technologies, the more rational minds move toward universal agreement on these issues. The extrapolations of scientists and logicians must be part of peace education efforts because this information helps motivate people to seek new answers to issues of safety and security. But scientific information is not and should not be the base of peace education. This information does not convince one to become peaceful. It only convinces one that old notions of safety and security are not working well. Fear of death, danger and scarcity still exist and can lead one to either more warlike or more peaceful conclusions about what to do about it.

This is why I am concerned mostly about the psychological and philosophical underpinnings of peace education. As we start to educate our young to seek peace, great attention must be paid to fundamental contextual issues less obvious than the threat of nuclear destruction. One such issue which I wish to highlight is the notion of relationship, of how relationships exist in nature and how relationships are most profitably conducted. I believe that a new understanding of relationship is the crucial foundation of successful peace education efforts. The children who are now in our families and in our schools will be faced with confounding decisions as adults. They will be forced to reevaluate the usefulness of many relational issues such as: individualism, competition, protection, nationalism, war, and personal attachment. To chart a peaceful future they will have to rethink the dualities of win-lose, love-hate and separate-whole.

It is a new understanding of relationships as explained to us, interestingly enough, by Albert Einstein, that I believe is the first block on which peace education efforts must be built. For example, we must educate our populace to the more complete significance of the discoveries of Einstein and his colleagues. For not only have Einsteinian insights pointed the way to the unleashing of the destructive power of the atom, they have also shown the way to a more accurate definition of life. By describing all matter including humans as truly related indivisible parts of the same whole and always influenced by the action of any component part, Einstein, I believe, has uncovered the path to species survival.

Unfortunately for the species, however, most humans have only accepted half of what Einstein discovered about the relationship of energy and matter. Finding that energy and matter are the same, we have been able to use that information to create weapons of unthinkable destructive power. Yet I believe that this knowledge also carries with it the potential for a golden age of social interactions. What we have to do is help people understand and act on that knowledge.

We who influence social policy, teach children, and design human services, along with our political and business leaders, including those who set national and international policy, act as if we still live in the world of Isaac Newton. The solutions we propose, our habits of thought and our world view reflect our ignorance of the physical universe. Much of what transpires in the domain of human interactions is based on definitions of reality that have been proven incomplete by the scientific discoveries of our times. Much of how the course of human events is plotted is based on inaccurate assumptions about how life really exists or resistance to truths already apparent.

Our habits keep us inclined to view matter as concrete, separate, distinct and objectively defined. Viewing reality this way leads one to focus on differences and search for boundaries. This type of thinking encourages notions of separation. It is no surprise then that, for the most part, humans have become parochial, partisan, separatists, looking out for themselves and their group, fortifying their boundaries against other groups and pursuing a path of acquisition of materials judged to be important to their survival and comfort. Most humans see their group goals as attainable at the expense of other groups and others' goals attainable at the expense of their goals. These social interaction concepts are descended from Newtonian concepts of reality, a reality that has been shown by particle and quantum physicists to be incomplete in its explanation of the universe. How differently humans might understand life if they were grounded in the knowledge of Einstein. For example, quantum physics has shown us that to see something as having an absolute identity is a perceptive differentiation on the part of the observer, a creative illusion and not a fact. We who live the world view of Isaac Newton create distinct identities by our own judgments and believe that what we create exists independent of our perceptions. We are inclined to concretize and objectify and we teach our offspring to do the same. Yet, from Einstein's viewpoint a person or an object is more accurately described not as a distinct identity -- a redhead, a Russian, a teacher or a table -- but as a wave in a universal ocean, identifiable by its form but part of, influenced by, and having influence on all other parts of that ocean.

These types of constructs if universally accepted would have a dramatic impact on relationships of all sorts. The following words of Jonas Salk (1983) are not just a nice way to think about life -- they are true. "It is to the advantage of everyone to enhance the best that exists in every individual for everyone's mutual benefit." (p.54) Seeing relationships in this new way gives less value to notions of opposition and unchangeable positions and more validity to notions of mutually advantageous relationships and shared connections. Science is telling us that all life is connected, and that an attack on part of life reverberates through all of life. Peace educators must build on this more accurate view of relationship and teach:

- The power of varied perspectives
- The importance of relationship to harmonious functioning
- The dependence of life on connections among living things
- The limitations of defining and objectifying too concretely

- The incompleteness of non-holistic explanations.

In practical terms this means emphasizing cooperative relationships and deemphasizing individual aggrandizement. This mode of reasoning about the world leads to obvious peace education activities and also to a conflict with the organizing world view that is now popular. We live in a time when the logic of how life might be safely lived is suddenly shifting. Some people have awakened to this shift while others think that the new logic threatens our safety. It is the job of peace educators to help people understand where security and safety now lie, to teach a new understanding of relationship. What follows are a few examples of lessons that need to be taught.

WE NEED TO BROADEN MULTICULTURAL EXPERIENCES FOR CHILDREN. Our children need to learn acceptance of people from other cultures. Children need experience in seeing their own culture and other cultures as complementary parts of the larger whole, not as rivals. There is an old saying, "All truth cannot be told in any one language." Our inclination to look at differences either as weakness or something to be feared has kept societies apart. After centuries of living on the same small planet, people from different cultures barely know each other. Why do we not teach our children respect for the creativity and dignity of other cultures? We now have the technology to bring to the eyes of our young the special ways people from different cultures view life. We must engage in non-partisan mind building. We must let children see that no one culture can claim exclusive rights to the truth and that people and societies can become more whole by learning of their connectedness to other cultures.

WE MUST TEACH AND MODEL A MORE RELATIONAL SENSE OF SELF. Let us rebalance definitions of identity to include one's connection with other life forms. Like a stone which makes concentric ripples outward when it is dropped in a pond, individual identity starts with self and moves outward to include connections with family, community, society, humans, all life itself, and finally all existence. This definition of self disinclines people to feelings of isolation and inclines people to feelings of shared experience. Individuality in our society has gone to destructive extremes. For each child to have separate toys, a separate room, etc., inclines the child to think that separateness is the natural and desirable condition and inclines the child to push for continued separateness as an adult.

WE MUST REDEFINE MENTAL HEALTH AND ACCEPTABLE BEHAVIOR IN HUMANS AND RAISE CHILDREN ACCORDINGLY. Rosemarie Greiner (1983) in a workshop she conducts on the foundations of peace education states that we should aim toward educating people so that they have:

- High levels of self awareness
- High levels of awareness of others
- High levels of imagination
- Sound conflict resolution skills
- Love of nature
- Global awareness

Mental health is not the absence of psychological problems, it is the presence of strong intellectual and emotional capacities and an understanding of the need for connections among people. We as a society now settle for too limited a notion of mental health.

WE MUST TEACH THE CONNECTIONS BETWEEN COOPERATION AND COMPETITION. THESE CONNECTIONS NEED TO BE EXPOUNDED AND EXPERIENCED BY CHILDREN SO THEY CAN LEARN THE ROLE OF LAWFULNESS AND INDIVIDUAL RESPONSIBILITY. Every game a child plays, every function in which a child participates, takes place within the context of a cooperative agreement, but for some strange reason we have failed to focus on this fact. Childhood can be a time when children see that their competitive joys remain joys only when there are laws to the competition, when the competition doesn't spill over the boundaries of the cooperative agreements and that there can be true loss in winning when competition goes too far. Children can understand the parallel to the game of life and the competition between nations.

WE MUST INSTITUTE SOCIALIZATION AND DISCIPLINE PRACTICES THAT ARE NON-VIOLENT AND DEVELOP THE CAPACITY FOR CONFLICT RESOLUTION IN THE CLASSROOM OR HOME. If we wield power in the old ways we will not be modeling the cooperation needed to solve world problems. We must teach children to search for solutions to conflict that leave the parties with self respect and shared ownership of the truth.

WE MUST CREATE AN EDUCATIONAL SETTING FILLED WITH HOPE. If life is to be sustained, hope must remain, even when confidence is wounded and trust impaired. Sybille Escalona (1982) has said that the nature of relations in today's world can cause widespread hopelessness. Erikson reminds us in Insight and Responsibility (1964) that in adults hope arises from the functional unity of love, work, homelife, friendship and citizenship. He also tells us that the rudiments of the virtues of hope, will, purpose and competence are developed in childhood. Hope is a particularly important virtue because without it, will, purpose and competence wane, and given what children now face, it is critical that they gain from their early experience a sense of hope. According to Erikson, hope is the enduring belief in the attainability of fervent wishes. Let us be inventive in creating centers of hope, for doing so is this generation's most important task. This is a developmental task that starts for a child in a healthy womb and delivery and follows with close connections with principal care-givers during the first months of life that maximize early feelings of personal security. It continues in an educational environment that sequentially optimizes the development of confidence, then initiative, followed by a sense of social responsibility leading toward a feeling of usefulness and potency.

WE MUST TEACH THE RELATIONSHIP BETWEEN A PERSONAL PEACE AND GLOBAL PEACE. Peace on earth may never come in our lifetime. Yet I am confident that those who pursue universal peace, international peace, national peace, civil peace, community peace and family peace must also practice personal peace. Personal peace taps the spiritual sources of life and connects the individual to creative energies. If one were to spend one's days in search of world peace without inner peace as a starting point and as a place to return, one would soon be moved to exhaustion and despair. Personal peace validates any larger quest for peace, for it shows the individual who experiences it that peace is possible, that it can be attained. When a person drops for a while the struggles of the day, stills the warring drives and deeply quiets, notions of separateness fade, and the "individual" finds himself or herself simply at peace, or more accurately "in peace." Inner peace can come in the most trying times, in any setting, as one surrenders to the experience of being at one with the life force.

If we wish to prepare children for peace in the fearful realities we have created, we must model peacefulness for them, establishing our own connections with the positive life-generating source in each of us. And we must provide opportunities for children to experience the source of renewal within themselves.

These are just a few examples of how a changed understanding of the power of relationship can serve peace education. But educators need to realize that this kind of teaching is as revolutionary as when Copernicus declared the sun, rather than the earth, to be the center of the solar system. We are suggesting that individuals, groups and nations radically change the way they view their own significance and relationship to each other, and many people see this work as heresy, as following a course of ultimate danger. We in peace education are calling on people to unlearn much of what they have learned with regard to survivial and security and to step into a new world view. We are asking them to make a Copernican change, to transform the relations between nations and individuals, themselves included.

Many people are unable to think in new ways about security and safety because those new ways seem to be in direct conflict with strategies that have worked for them in the past and in which they have been trained. We must not lose sight of the fact that survival concepts of the past served a valuable function and are in fact the scaffolding that facilitates the construction of new survival concepts. People will not leave the scaffolding and step into a new building if they think the building is unsafe, so we must demonstrate the safety of the new construction.

I am convinced that peace education efforts can be successful if we can help people understand the true value of supportive relationships. This is not an easy task, but I believe there is no alternative. Like it or not we live in a world made different by the discoveries of physics and we need to see the benefit of these discoveries in addition to their dangers. Einstein (1946) himself counseled:

> ...just as we have changed our thinking in the world of pure science to embrace newer and more useful concepts, so we must now change our thinking in the world of politics and law. It is too late to make mistakes...past thinking and methods did not succeed in preventing world wars. Future thinking must prevent wars.

It is the job of peace educators to educate citizens in the concepts that will prevent war and to help children develop the character they will need to live in the world they will inherit.

REFERENCES

Commager, H. "Foreign Policy: Outmoded Assumptions." *Atlantic Monthly*, Mar. 1982.

Einstein, A. *The Meaning of Relativity*. Princeton University Press: 1945.

"Only Then Shall We Find Courage." *The New York Times Magazine*, June 23, 1946.

Erikson, E. *Insight and Responsibility*. New York: W.W. Norton, 1964.

Escalona, S. "Growing Up with the Threat of Nuclear War: Some Indirect Effects on Personality Development." Presented at the Symposium: Preparing for Nuclear War: The Psychological Effects. New York. Feb. 13, 1982.

Greiner, R. *Peace Education: A Bibliography Focusing on Young Children*. Greiner. 126 Escalona Dr., Santa Cruz, CA 65060

Salk, J. "A Conversation with Jonas Salk." *Psychology Today*. March, 1983.

APPROACHING THE NUCLEAR THREAT IN CLINICAL WORK WITH CHILDREN AND THEIR FAMILIES

John E. Mack, M.D.

How in clinical work do we deal with the threat of nuclear war? This subject has been very little attended to in the field of psychiatry. We know little about how the nuclear threat manifests itself in the clinical situation. How do clinicians deal with the issue when it does show up? Do they recognize it, and, if so, how do they recognize it? How should they deal with it? I'm going to start with the assumption that the great body of clinicians, the thousands of clinicians that work with children, deal with this issue very little, if at all. I will consider some possible reasons.

One reason might be that it is not appropriate for the psychiatrist or other clinician, that it does not come up, and that it really does not belong to the clinician's domain. But right away we can answer that we know of cases. A psychiatrist, Joseph Shoulders, from Napa, California, wrote me about the case of an eleven-year-old son of a nuclear engineer whose three named wishes, in a routine evalution, were 1) to eliminate all nuclear weapons, including the ability to create them, 2) for all planets in the solar system to be like resorts, and 3) to have a copy of all the books ever published. This boy, a gifted straight A student, turned out in later discussions to have a lingering and pervasive terror of nuclear war. Robert Simon, a family therapist, reports:

> A 20-year-old college student suffering from panic attacks recounted the following dream, "I know that the house is on fire or that we are being robbed. I go downstairs where there is a large crowd of family and friends, and I try to warn them. But everybody acts as though nothing is happening. After a while I start to think I'm crazy."

In clinical work with children and adolescents we are dealing with questions about the future, about goals, possibilities and relationships between individuals and groups of people, all of which are deeply affected by the nuclear context and the threat of nuclear annhiliation.

A second possible reason that we do not deal with this issue has to do with the fact that we do not have an appropriate theory. My own background is that of an old-think Freudian analyst and psychologist, and that tradition is weak in theories about human psychological functioning that connect individual experience with the impact of phenomena in the external world. We know a good deal, at the family level -- the impact, for example, of family relationships as represented by family introjects. But what is the effect of living with the continuing threat or possibility of annihilation? Without a theory of how a threat in the larger world, the macrocosm, can show up in individual psychological functioning, it is difficult to notice matters related to the nuclear threat, even if they are, in fact, present.

Our understanding of psychological functioning has occurred in relation to a set of phenomena about which we have a theory, like intra-psychic conflict or interpersonal relations in families. So it is possible that the nuclear threat is affecting our patients, but that we do not have a way to notice this in clinical practice. For instance, the patterns of avoidance around the nuclear threat might look different to us if we felt the nuclear threat could be important. If a patient says, for example, "I don't get into politics," we have tended to accept it as a neutral statement, responding perhaps with, "Okay, you don't get into politics, now tell me what you do get into." But if we see that statement as a defense, meaning, "I'm afraid around being responsible politically," and we think it is important to look at such a statement as a kind of defense, we might use a different approach. Through free association we wait for topics to show up, or we may have dialogues with patients, but it may be that in this area a different kind of responsibility and initiative is required for the therapist in order to bring forth something which is taboo culturally as well as psychologically. Robert Simon gives the example of asking a man in a family meeting, "What are your fears about the future?" This man then listed the nuclear danger as his greatest fear. But the subject had not come up spontaneously in weeks of family work.

A third reason the nuclear threat might not be expressed is that the therapist has yet to confront his or her own anxieties and political points of view. We probably have a lot of homework to do in this area, and it is not just the usual kind of homework. It has to do with our whole relationship to the world in which we live, our society, our view of politics and international relations and where we take a stand, our careers, who might criticize us, all that "political" stuff. I use the word political because I think that is really what is involved. The nuclear weapons problem is not only a psychological matter, but it is a political problem involving our selves as political beings, which most of us are not accustomed to acknowledging in a highly intentioned way. So we have homework on our political selves to do.

Some mental health clinicians do not think this subject belongs in the mental health field. In the Congressional hearings on children's fears of war, there was testimony from a psychiatrist from the Menninger Clinic who was opposed to nuclear education programs in the schools on the grounds that educators would be trying to put forth their political views. Whether you agree with him or not, he is a psychiatrist at Menninger Clinic, which is a reputable place, and, presumably, this is what he is telling his trainees and patients. He says,

> Bluntly put, these programs can only scare the wits out of young people, challenge them with unsolvable problems, provoke a reaction of despair and hopelessness, ultimately leading to a sense of hopelessness about the future, and possibly result in reaction to aggression of any kind. Remember, there is nothing inherently evil about force or aggression - rather, the purpose for which aggression is used can be evil. Children may not and probably cannot grasp that distinction. Even mature men tend to renounce all aggresssion after prolonged exposure to it. A few children might become excessively aggressive as a reaction to this material.

Is this not a political point of view? This man speaks from the heartland of America, from the Midwest.

Those are some of the ideas I have about why we do not talk about the nuclear issue in clinical work. Now, let us turn to the subject itself. One person who has done some very interesting studies on this subject is Adela Wilkeson, a psychiatrist who has been working at McLean Hospital in Boston. She found that in her work with on-going adult therapy cases, she needed to deal with the nuclear threat in 11 out of 16 cases. So she asked herself, how come? She did not find any literature on this. She was aware that it had something to do with her own relation to the subject, her own awareness. She found the discussions with her patients to be of therapeutic value. She was able to deal with anxieties related to the nuclear threat and in doing so forwarded the work on other issues. There was a short-term increase in anxiety in her patients, but, over-all, addressing nuclear issues moved the therapy forward. Therapeutic progress did involve the patient's undertaking some activity in the area of disarmament, or work related to the nuclear issue. I know of no other systematic reports like Wilkeson's. She is now developing a questionnaire to be given to thousands of therapists to explore what relationship there is between the attitude of the therapist on the points I brought up earlier and what shows up clinically in work with patients.

I will now tell you in somewhat more detail about an eleven-year-old girl I saw myself in 1982. I met with Lisa twice and with her parents separately. I also have had some follow-up information about her. Lisa came to see me because she had asked her mother whether in the interval between learning that nuclear weapons were on their way and the time of detonation there would be time to commit suicide. The parents, who are professional people, were obviously very troubled about this, and as I was then the "nuclear fear" psychiatrist in the area, she ended up being brought to see me. Lisa is an attractive, gifted, intelligent child, especially sensitive to world problems, precocious and artistic. She loves horses and has a good deal of rivalry with her older sister. She was a wanted baby and is an affectionate child. Starting about the third grade, when Lisa was nine, she began to have a number of fears and nightmares about monsters, and guilt over "bad thoughts," which she told her parents that she deserved. At the time I saw her there was also a beginning interest in boys and Lisa told stories of what was happening between boys and girls at her school. Her parents were concerned that although they had attempted to shield Lisa from all of the violent, distressing news in the world, she was now especially interested in learning about such matters on her own and they worried that they could not protect her.

I was particularly interested in what Lisa had to say because I had not seen a child with this sort of complaint before. We talked about other subjects, but what follows are comments of hers that seemed related to our topic. Our meetings were tape recorded. In the first session, Lisa said, "I worry a lot about people dying. Nuclear war. I worry a lot about that. That's more reasonable than worrying about ghosts and monsters and things, but it's still not exactly pleasant. I think a lot about nuclear war and everything scary when it's dark and my thoughts aren't quite together...Sometimes it just seems that everything is dark and dismal and I'm sure the Russians are going to launch a bomb...I like reading the news and finding out what's happening and I don't like to be told that, 'Oh, it's all okay' and all that, because sometimes it's not. About nuclear war and things like that. I mean when you know things. Sometimes when I'm thinking reasonably, I'm less scared. I realize how unlikely it is that anyone would launch an attack because it's so ghastly. Nobody wants to have themselves attacked right back again. Well, nuclear war isn't something that seeps in the window and gets you. It's reasonable. It's politics. It's real life, not like some of the things you hear about, like a tape of the Black Cat, that just couldn't be. I know it's impossible. Those are the things I worry about. I don't know why I worry about them. But a nuclear war is possible, so it's a little more depressing than it is scary. It's scary in a different way. Not like it's haunting. It's like it might come down and kill thousands of people." Lisa repeatedly made the distinction between things that are real, out there, and fears related to her conflicts with her parents, her rivalries, impulses and fantasies.

I asked Lisa if she thought that children think about political problems. She said, "Some do. I think there are lots of different types of children. I think most of the kids I know, if you ask them their greatest fear, it would be nuclear war. I mean everybody, all kids, are scared to death that they won't live to be thirty. Most of the kids in my school (an elementary school in a well-to-do suburb of Boston) are scared. I'm almost sure that all of them are, except the really, really dumb ones. I don't think they care, because if it's not happening right now then they don't understand. They think, well, it might happen, but as long as they're safe watching the television, then it's okay with them. A minority of the kids...think, well, there can't be a war, that stuff's what you read in the newspaper, and (they) sit down and watch The Dukes of Hazzard and that will clear it up." It was important for Lisa to be in charge of the situation, to have control when the issue had to do with politics or real things. Lisa felt troubled in a different way by "unreal" things where knowledge and control didn't help, "other fears, like a skeleton is going to be creaking at the door and things like that. It all just takes too much of my time."

Lisa said, "My imagination scares me. Even when my imagination isn't running away, I can still be scared of death and things like that. So that's one of the things that scares me most...I'm still scared of being killed when I'm unreasonable, so I figure that's still a reasonable thought, even when it's, well, unreasonable, 'cause it still deals with death and death is something that I consider to be sort of reasonable, 'cause it happens. I can't really categorize it into what is real death and what couldn't be. In Social Studies, that's really the only thing you worry about --nuclear war, the countries building up arms, defense, nuclear peace demonstrations and riots and other things like that. That's what they deal with basically. Relationships between countries and the feud between Iran, the PLO and all that. So you really can't help it."

I wondered why she in particular seemed so worried about nuclear war. "I guess that I just have more access to it," Lisa said. "Other people just don't seem to understand anything about it. They sit at home; they watch The Dukes of Hazzard. That's all they ever do. They don't read the paper. They don't find out about things like that. Reading the paper you learn a lot of interesting things. You also learn a lot about death, because I'm more exposed to it. My mother says that I'm imaginative in good ways and creative and it has to be the other way around. Anybody who's imaginative, who's really creative and all that has to be in the other direction, too." Lisa and I agreed she was suffering a lot from her fears, and that they were complicated.

I discussed with Lisa's parents the complex mixture of real fears and pre-adolescent conflict, the possible displacement of other fears onto the nuclear threat, and the interrelationship between this threat and her private conflicts. I had to acknowledge, however, the impact of the nuclear reality on their daughter and what it meant to her. They did not seem to want to hear this. They preferred to look upon her difficulties as those of a conventional neurotic conflict, to be brought to a child therapist who could deal with them in ways that were more familiar. They took Lisa to two other therapists. She did not stay with either of them. I spoke with one of them, who said that Lisa had a phobic problem, and when he talked with her about other conflicts, her nuclear fears faded.

One and a half years later, in preparation for a conference on the nuclear issue in child psychiatry, I called up Lisa's mother to see how things were going. Lisa was now almost thirteen. Her mother said that Lisa was not expressing her nuclear fears, but listening to hard rock groups and watching violent late night videos, while she was trying to get Lisa to listen to Beethoven. Lisa wasn't interested in that. She had become cynical about society and its mass violence and would say to her mother, for example, when she was raising money for a campaign for mitral stenosis, "What's the use?" The mother said that Lisa seemed to be at the mercy of "external forces". Five days later the mother called me back on her own. She said that that week Lisa had a nightmare about nuclear war and could not sleep. Lisa asked if Canada would be destroyed in a nuclear war. "I said, 'probably.' 'South America?' I said,'Probably not.' 'Australia?' I said, 'Probably not.' 'Could we move to Australia?' Lisa asked. I said, 'Oh, Lisa, I'm not going to let anything happen to you.' Lisa said, 'Oh, you can't stop it.' Then she told the nightmare and said she has a lot of fantastic dreams, that she thinks about nuclear war all the time, that there's nothing to be said or done about it, so why talk about it." Her mother told me, "I lie all the time to her. Since 1945, we've had it (the bomb). I say to her, 'We'll go another forty years, and no one will push the trigger,' I say, but that's not what I really think. The alternative is to wipe her out, so that's why I lie. I never tell a factual lie. After all there is a possibility Australia might escape."

What does this case illustrate? First, this is an unusual child. Lisa brings the nuclear subject up in the teeth of the resistance of the parents and the society. But she remains alone with it. She makes distinctions between the fears that reside primarily within her psychological developmental conflicts and real things that are "out there". Lisa seeks help with that distinction. She reflects the difficulty that therapists and parents have with this issue. We see the relationship between the nuclear weapons problem and pre-adolescent conflicts about control, separation, excitement and aggression. Lisa's worries go underground because there is no receptivity in her environment, particularly from her parents, which would enable her to give them expression.

Lisa has great difficulty bringing her distress about the nuclear issue to her parents. When she does bring it to her mother, her mother lies, not out of a lack of feeling for Lisa, but because she herself feels helpless to protect the child, to do anything constructive for her. This case also illustrates the enormous power in our mass media-dominated world, that the external threats communicated by the media can have on the psychological life of young people. Lisa's case makes us wonder again about the massive impact of external threats on the development of young people, especially children who are not as articulate as Lisa.

Lisa herself, in pulling back into her autistic world of hard rock and violent videos, is already showing some effect of the nuclear world, and of her parents' inability to come to terms with it, upon her developing adolescent personality.

In my concluding remarks, I want to comment on the family dimensions of this matter. Sybille Escalona has observed that children are rarely offered examples of adults behaving responsibly in relation to the nuclear threat. For the first time in the literature of family therapy, there are now a few papers emerging which address how the nuclear threat is being dealt with in families. Robert Simon and Steve Zeitlin, family therapists writing in the journal, <u>The Family Therapy Networker</u>, have expressly examined this problem. Simon calls it a collective family secret. The issue is overwhelming for families, for individual children and their parents. Through interviews with a number of families, they found that a silent compact becomes established between the children and their parents. The children do not want to disturb their parents and the parents do not want to trouble the children, but for different reasons. "Without permission to raise concerns, our children will continue to protect us," Zeitlin writes. "When this happens, I believe children are robbed of a sense of well-being." The children often say, in effect, I don't want to trouble my parents because I know my parents can't do anything about it and they can't handle it. This raises profound questions about the sense of futurelessness and its impact on families as a whole.

What can we recommend? There are no easy answers. It would be useful to acknowledge our ignorance about how to deal with this subject clinically. It is highly sensitive politically and there is no way to get around the fact that we are confronting our political beliefs, our political selves, when we address this issue. For example, if we believe that more weapons are needed for a strong defense, then it would be important to notice how that shows up in the work that we do with our clients.

Also what exposure should children have to nuclear reality? There is a balance somewhere between knowledge which is useful and knowledge which is overwhelming. What should clinicians offer in the way of possibilities for change, by, for instance, providing examples of themselves and other adults acting responsibly in relation to the nuclear dilemma? There is a variety of possible and appropriate responses. But therapists need to be prepared to deal with this issue in one way or another. The topic is taboo, somewhat like the subject of sexual abuse just a few years ago. As was found in research on sexual matters, when the therapist asks questions, or is open to the fact that the issue is appropriate and important, material will show up in clinical sessions, as Adela Wilkeson's research has shown. How should we deal with the children themselves? How do we find out when they are troubled about the nuclear threat? They will not necessarily tell us. The distress may be masked, as in Lisa's case, behind a fixation on violent videos or hard rock, which sometimes express themes of nuclear annihilation and futurelessness. How do we deal with the fears of parents? Some of you are beginning to have workshops with parents and thinking through with them how to take this subject up with their kids, so they will not have to feel, as Lisa's parents did, that they have no choice but to lie. How do we see our role as consultants to teachers? What do we say about nuclear education? How do we feel about talking about the Russians in the schools? How do we work with school administrators and boards and with the political structures of our communities around the subject of nuclear education?

What it really seems to come to is this: it would be helpful to give young people a chance to see adults acting responsibly on this issue, being involved in some way -- not necessarily having the answers but asking useful questions. Perhaps you know Judith Lipton's wonderful example of the teacher in Seattle who asked her class of fifteen second graders, "How many of you think there's going to be a nuclear war?" Fourteen out of fifteen raised their hands and so she asked the fifteenth child, "Why don't you think so?" "My parents go to meetings where they talk about nuclear war and how to prevent it," the child replied. Clearly, the painful conspiracy of silence in families has to be addressed. We need to work closely with parents and think through with them how to discuss this problem meaningfully and appropriately.

Finally, we do need to protect our children, not by denying the issue or lying to them, but by preparing them for the world that they are living in. I will close with a statement by Steve Zeitlin: "If we really prepare our children to live in the world, they do not lose their childhood. We have an opportunity to give the gift of trustworthiness to our children, by acknowledging with them that the threat of nuclear war has a significant effect on our lives, and by taking personal responsibility for working within our beliefs to make the world safe. But if we fail to protect and fail to prepare, then not only have our children lost their childhood, but we will also lose our parenthood."

REFERENCES

Children's Fears of War. Hearing before the Select Committee on Children, Youth and Families, September 20, 1983. U.S. Government Printing Office, 1984.

Simon, Robert. "The Nuclear Family." The Family Therapy Networker, March/April, 1984

Wilkeson, Adela. "Nuclear Arms: Psychiatrists' Professional Role." Material from Dr. Wilkeson's studies has been presented at the Annual Meeting of the American Academy of Psychotherapists and at other professional conferences.

Zeitlin, Steven. The Family Therapy Networker, March/April, 1984

THE POLITICAL PSYCHOLOGY OF DETERRENCE

Richard Smoke, Ph.D.

Although I have done work with psychology -- several years at the Wright Institute in Berkeley -- I am basically a political scientist by training, and I feel a little bit like the token arms control and disarmament expert in this environment, a role I enjoy. My charge is to talk about the psychology of deterrence.

When we saw the videotaped interviews with families, I was struck, as I think we all were, by the manifest fear of the children, but there's nothing surprising about this at all, because the whole idea of deterrence is based on fear. The very concept of deterrence, whether it is used in the international context, or whether we're talking about, for example, a prison sentence as a deterrent against crime, is by its very nature based on the idea of a threat, on the idea that you must inspire fear in those whom you wish to deter. The word <u>deterrence</u> has the same root as the word <u>terror</u>. So the very nature of deterrence involves fear.

There is also nothing new about the idea of deterrence in international affairs, but there is something quite new in the way deterrence has been used since World War II. Prior to World War II, the concept of deterrence in international relations referred to one side threatening war against the other side's military forces. Deterrence was a game that was played at the level of capitals, at the level of political elites, at the level of military commanders and military forces, but <u>not</u> at the level of populations. The threat to civilian populations began with the strategic bombing campaigns of World War II and was developed and refined in the nuclear age to become the problem that we have now. The concept of deterrence is largely a creature of the nuclear age and is a product of the unbelievable destructiveness of nuclear weapons.

By about 1955 there was in this country something called a national security expert; not a general, not a politician, but a wholly new creation which had never existed before. People of that sort, like the physicist Herman Kahn, for example, have engaged in a great deal of deterrence theorizing, producing a highly developed literature and set of theories based on the logic of political science, military science, economics or physics, not on the logic of psychology. Deterrence policy in the West, and I think in the Soviet Union as well, has not been developed by psychologists and has not been carried out with any attention to the broader psychological implications of that policy. It is as if, unconsciously, all these theorists were still thinking in the old terms, that deterrence is a game played by governments and their military forces, even though the new reality is that whole populations are being threatened. No one looked at the question of what might be the psychological ramifications of deterrence policies for people as a whole, just as nobody wondered about the climactic effects of blasting 100,000 tons of smoke into the atmosphere. We only discovered the possibility of nuclear winter last year, not because we couldn't have thought of it sooner, but because people simply weren't looking at that kind of question.

The American deterrence policy began shortly after World War II, originally as an effort to deter the possibility of a Soviet ground attack against Western Europe, in the days when only the United States had nuclear weapons. After World War II, all the Western European countries completely disarmed, but the Soviet Union did not completely disarm and there continued to be a huge Red Army in Eastern Europe. An expression that was famous in those days was, "All the Russians need is shoes, to march to the English Channel." The American deterrence policy originated to prevent Soviet invasion of Western Europe by a first implicit, later explicit, threat that should such a thing occur, the Soviet Union would be atomic bombed in response.

Within a year after the explosion of the first Soviet nuclear weapon, an important doctrine was conceived in Washington called NSC-68, which introduced the idea that the two sides' nuclear forces would balance and deter each other. That has been the idea of deterrence since.

The Korean War provided a corollary to deterrence theory in that it was taken by many of these so-called national security experts to be proof that it was impossible for the two sides to fight small-scale wars with each other by proxy, "under the nuclear umbrella." The nuclear deterrent relationship was seen as being so stable, so powerful, in a sense so good, that you could even have a war and it wouldn't threaten that balance.

Deterrence was further codified under the Kennedy Administration by Robert MacNamara and his crew of Whiz Kids in the Pentagon. It was first called Assured Destruction and shortly thereafter modified to the doctrine of Mutually Assured Destruction, when the Soviet Union achieved striking power that could level the United States as readily as the United States had been able to level the Soviet Union for quite a while. So, through a series of steps, deterrence came to mean that the two sides' strategic nuclear forces deter each other in a stable relationship, that the whole thing works because it is technically and militarily sound, and that we can ignore whatever might be deeper and more humanistic implications.

At this point, we may have some possibility of breaking out of that confined cognitive space, partly as a result of the peace movement and partly as a result of precisely the kind of work this conference is drawing attention to. The evidence is accumulating that in deterrence policy there are serious long-term implications for the mental health of the entire planet.

Our children are perhaps especially sensitive, and, as others at this conference are suggesting, we get some of the most vivid evidence from them, but we should also be aware of the mental health damage to the entire adult population. In both the Soviet Union and the United States, there is, increasingly, a shared recognition of the psychological danger of the nuclear threat, and, therefore, I think we have a possibility of breaking out of the deterrent mind set.

Let me say parenthetically that there are the strangest paradoxes in the strategic theorizing on arms control. One of the things that comes up, for example, among conservatives, is the following kind of reasoning: that precisely because both sides are increasingly appreciating the mutual danger of nuclear war, therefore the other guy should start disarming. One of the things that happens in the logic of this field is that arguments which appear to be going one way get turned around and used the other way. In my judgment, there really was a political, even cynical, effort on the part of the Soviet Union in 1983 to appeal to the immense idealistic, peace-seeking impulse in Western Europe in order to shift the focus of Western European protest from Soviet deployments to American deployments. The United States, to some extent, has done the same thing. In Strobe Talbot's recent book, Deadly Gambits, which is basically a history of the arms control efforts of the last four years (both at the strategic level and with respect to the European issues), he points out time and time again how people in Washington sit down and actually ask themselves questions like, "How can we use the political impulse, the political will, the political energy of the peace movement and turn it to the American advantage in terms of the on-going competition with the Soviet Union?" There is a continuing tendency in both capitals to take the energy that is created by all those who are deeply concerned about the danger to us all and turn it to a unilateral, nationalistic purpose.

Looking now at a slightly different aspect of the psychology of deterrence, I believe that the extent to which the ongoing deterrent relationship has serious psychological consequences depends, not just on the existence of a large number of warheads on both sides, but also on the political relationship of the two sides at any given time, and on what appears to be the longer-term trend. The peace movement burgeoned in the West in 1981 and 1982, whereas in 1979, when many of the experts were extremely eager to get popular support for the Salt II treaty, there was not much interest among the American public. The increased interest in 1981 and 1982 can be partly explained as an immediate reaction to some very foolish statements that were made by the Reagan administration, to some very irresponsible policies. I think another part of it was a widespread apprehension that the long-term trend was turning downward both with respect to the dangers represented by the weapons themselves and the overall Soviet-American relationship. To a considerable extent, the population as a whole does not so much react to given events or given speeches or given decisions as it does to a general impression of whether relations between world powers are proceeding in a positive or a negative direction.

Another reason why the peace movement was so active in '81 and '82 is that for awhile there had been no serious negotiations going on between East and West on arms control issues. The power of the peace movement, particularly in Western Europe, began to ebb away when negotiations began, which, incidentally, was one of the motivations for opening the negotiations. I have heard leaders of the peace movement criticize the arms control experts on the grounds that, not only is arms control fundamentally not succeeding, but that, to the extent that it appears to be making some progress, the public stops paying attention -- that, as it were, the arms control enterprise is lulling the public to sleep while we drive to Armageddon.

This is not to say that I'm opposed to arms control, but I wish to draw your attention to the way in which the psychological meaning of deterrence is dependent on the public's impression of the long-term trend. Suppose, for example, that in the next few years Moscow and Washington were able to define a situation in the future that they could aim toward that would be safer, let's say a defined U.S.-Soviet relationship and a defined level of disarmament, for the year 1995, for example. And suppose they then reasoned backwards from that image of what they wanted 1995 to look like in order to define what should be negotiated now or in 1987 or 1989. If there was something positive in the future that both sides were working toward, that would change the psychology of the situation dramatically. In spite of the fact that between now and 1995 the deterrent situation would continue, and a certain basic threat of being able to destroy each other's cities might continue even beyond that, my guess is that levels of anxiety among both children and adults would drop. The meaning of deterrence would be changed, because the trend would appear to be going in a positive direction. The psychology of deterrence is bound up with this larger collective judgment as to whether history, broadly speaking, is moving in a positive direction or a negative direction.

It is my hope that raising the issue, in the way that this conference and related efforts are raising the issue, will have a powerful effect on the way in which governments are dealing with this question, precisely because deterrence theorists have never really addressed the larger psychological implications of deterrence policy. It's becoming fairly clear that it is psychologically deleterious to maintain this kind of thing decade after decade after decade. Just as the nuclear winter findings have made an end run around all the elaborate "sophisticated" strategizing that's gone on about "survivable" nuclear war, so this kind of effort can end run much of the impulse behind deterrence by coming at the problem from an angle that the deterrence theorists themselves have never really addressed. Practically everybody has or knows children and everybody can come to understand that we and our children cannot sustain the harmful psychological effects of deterrence forever. This represents a hole in deterrence theory big enough to drive an ICBM through, which must lead to a recognition that deterrence cannot be with us forever. We have to find better solutions, and we can.

Reports on Research Findings

EXPLORING YOUTH'S REACTION TO THE THREAT OF NUCLEAR WAR

Jeffrey Gould, M.D.

What we want to do next is to give some of the evidence that the threat of nuclear war is actually having an impact on children. Three of us will briefly present the results of our respective research studies: myself, Judith Van Hoorn, and Tytti Solantaus.

The work that I'll be reporting on was done with the Nuclear Ecology Research Project.* You have all seen Vivienne Verdon Roe's film, "In the Nuclear Shadow: What Can the Children Tell Us?" The research I want to present really addresses three questions. The first is: Do worried children on the film represent children in general or are they a handful of carefully selected children who don't represent your children or mine? That's the first question. The second question is: If these children are representative of our children in a general sense, is this really what they have to say about the state of things, or has the interview situation got them psyched up and anxious and star struck so that they're saying things that they ordinarily wouldn't feel? And the third concern we wanted to address is: If children feel that the future of the world is so precarious, how do they prepare for their own future?

* The principal investigators were Eve Eden, Benina Berger Gould and myself, and the people who gave us invaluable help with scoring and getting the instrument together were Carol Oppenheimer, Leslie Knutson, Cathy Costello and Sarah Rosenthal.

To put it another way, is there a link between the feelings of dread we've heard expressed in the film, and certain pathologies that some people say are reaching epidemic proportions, such as teenage suicide, which increased by 136% between 1960 and 1980? These are the three basic questions.

We were thinking about how to look at this issue when the Korean airliner was shot down in August of '83. Because we were reviewing the literature, we decided that it would be appropriate to repeat a study that was referred to earlier, that Milton Schwebel did, following the Berlin Wall crisis in 1961. He asked children three very simple questions: Do you think there will be a war? Do you care, and why? What do you think about fallout shelters? We liked this format as a way to answer the questions I just mentioned, because Schwebel's questions are open-ended. However, we assumed that we would only get "yes," "no," "maybe," and a few little brief responses.

These questions were presented to school children by their teachers, in Maine, Minnesota, Massachusetts, and California, in the following way. The teacher would come into the room and say, "A great deal is known about how world leaders and adults feel about nuclear war. This survey will help us to learn what students feel about nuclear war. There will be three questions. We will take six minutes to answer each question. I will tell you when five minutes have gone by. If you need more paper, raise your hand." Each student is given two sheets of paper and the teacher states, "Here is question number one. Please write it down." The question is then repeated and the students instructed to begin. The three questions are: 1) Do I think there will be a war? 2) Do I care? Why? 3) What do I think about fallout shelters?

We received responses from over 1700 children, starting at the fourth grade and going up to the twelfth grade. The youngest group was the smallest and consisted of 60 fourth and fifth graders.

The first study that we did was of 256 ninth graders, so we could compare their responses to those obtained by Schwebel in 1961. These children were of mixed ability and from varied backgrounds, politically and socio-economically. They attended classes where the nuclear issue had either not been discussed or had only rarely or informally been discussed. They had not been part of any special nuclear education project or peace curriculum.

We found that following the Korean airliner incident, 64% of the children felt that there would be a war, as compared to 44% after the Berlin crisis. The difficulty with this figure is, how do we make it seem real to people? It's a number -- 64 -- what does that mean? What that means is that if you ask three children if there's going to be a war, two of those children are going to say, "Yeah, we do think there's going to be a war." One of the biggest difficulties I've had is making that 64% important to people. Could you imagine what would happen if the school bus drives up to your house, and three children get off and two of those children say, "The ride is nice, but I think I'm going to get killed on that bus." That would have a real impact on a community. You can imagine the telephones ringing, the mayor holding hearings, and all kinds of things.

An interesting aspect of our study was that when we started to read the responses, we were amazed at how much the students had written -- long responses, which we felt were probably the things that were really on their minds. So we then spent about seven months figuring out a 132 item content analysis that would allow us to characterize these responses. For example, to the question "Will there be a war," they didn't usually just say yes, they'd say yes, because of something. They might refer to when it would come, they'd sometimes blame. The content analysis is based on what they said.

We then compared the responses of three age groups: fourth-fifth graders, ninth graders and twelfth graders, to see if there was a developmental trend. As to the first question, 49% of fourth-fifth graders, 69% of ninth and 65% of twelfth graders felt there'd be a war. That's not a very significant difference. But there was a change in terms of their references to time. Only 4.5% of the younger children refer to time, but 55% of the twelfth graders make specific reference to time, with comments like, "It's going to happen soon," or "It's going to happen in my lifetime." So expectation of war stays stable, but reference to time increases as adulthood approaches.

As a sidelight, I'd like to mention that in an inner city situation, or in a classroom of disadvantaged children, we have observed that you get the same content as from a more privileged group, but the responses tend to be shorter. They might say there will be a war because "countries are at each other." In a more affluent setting, the children might say, "There's danger from increasing international tension." When you distill the content, it's about the same.

The children who said there was going to be a war cited world tension as the reason more than any other. Over all, approximately 45% of the children cited various specific kinds of world tension. Interestingly, the very crisis that precipitated our study, the Korean airline incident, was mentioned only 17% of the time, and this is in a study that was done within two weeks after the downing of the 007, at a time when vodka was being poured down drains, when liquor stores wouldn't stock Russian vodka. Fatalistic responses, such as "Man is a warring creature," or "War always happens," were given by only a very small percentage of the children who said there was going to be a war.

The children who said there was not going to be a war listed a variety of reasons, which fall into two general categories: the negative reasons -- war is awful, no one would do this, deterrence -- and the positive reasons -- man is looking toward the future and won't let this happen.

When asked, "Do you care, and why?" 95% of the children said that they cared, the same as in Schwebel's study. The first thing that they mention is loss, and total loss, global loss -- the whole world would be wiped out, the species will end, there won't be anything left of us -- was the most commonly cited. Loss of family or community we considered not as global loss, but as community loss; and community could be all of the state of California. When we're talking global, we're talking global, and 38% of the students refer to global loss. An interesting finding is that while some people say today's children are narcissistic, nevertheless, self-loss, "my loss," "my future," was only mentioned by 15% of the children. Only a small percentage of children (22%) expressed blame, saying its Reagan's fault or it's the Russian's fault or someone's fault, but twice as many ninth graders did so as either older or younger children. One of the biggest surprises, to us, was that an equal number of children (24%) talked about humanitarianism. Humanitarianism would be in a statement such as, "War is awful, of course I care, innocent people will be killed. It would be a terrible thing for the future of everybody." A frequent humanitarian response to fallout shelters was, "Even if fallout shelters work, there wouldn't be enough fallout shelters for everybody and so I think that they're a bad idea." So this emergence of humanitarianism was something that we didn't expect and was very, very touching.

One of the things that we felt was disappointing was the lack of solutions offered. Few fourth and fifth graders offer spontaneous solutions at all, and by the twelfth grade only 21% offer solutions. Based on this observation, we think that our questionnaire might be very good at evaluating so-called peace curricula. We would expect that as a result of a peace curriculum, the kind of curriculum that Ron Lally talks about, we would get many more spontaneous solutions offered than we saw in this particular study, even though we might not get major shifts in whether children worry about the possibility of war.

We wanted to look at the developmental aspect of the responses, with our comparison of the three age groups, and we found that the expectation of war was stable. But references to time increased as the children got older, as did references to loss, and suggested solutions.

So as the children get older, certain things stay stable, certain things increase and, very interestingly, there may be a ninth grade peak around the expression of blame, helplessness, and a belief in the efficacy of fallout shelters. In this particular study, we only evaluate 62 ninth graders, so it could be a sampling error, but it could be that this ninth grade peak really represents a kind of turning point. If you look at Ron Doctor's and John Goldenring's work, if you listen to Tytti Solantaus' reports from Finland, it appears that older students state that while they perceive the likelihood of war as being just as high, they worry less about it. Perhaps the peak of affectual responses seen in ninth graders represents an important step in a developmental coping strategy that tends to turn off affect and worry, a developmental coping strategy that results in nuclear disactivism, Lifton's "psychic numbing" as a developmental process.

We believe that several important speculations have emerged from our findings.

1) The high number of students who feel that nuclear war will occur and describe its devastation indicates that this is an important area for research.
2) The low number of students who cite the international crisis that occurred two weeks preceding the survey may indicate that adaptive psychologic mechanisms which result in blunting the perception of the importance of social/political events to the nuclear issue may be operative.
3) The low number of students who offer solutions to the threat of nuclear war may indicate that our educational and social system may not be preparing youth for an active role in the democratic process.

4) The findings that responses show differing maturational patterns suggest that a developmental process underlies youth's thoughts and feelings about growing up in a nuclear ecology.

At the beginning of this presentation I said that we hoped that our research would help to answer three questions. Are the children that we see in the film representative of all our own children, are they really telling us how they feel, and do these feelings have importance for their future development and well being? What we are discovering in the Nuclear Ecology Research Project is that the frightened children that we have seen on film are not a handful of carefully selected children, but that the children in our study from Maine and California, poor and rich, gifted and non-gifted, are saying the same things that were said by the children in the film, and in fact they say the same thing as the children in Dr. Schwebel's 1961 study, almost word for word, as he quotes them in his original article. So we're convinced at this point that the children we see on the films and in interview situations are our children in the broadest sense.

Secondly, we feel that because our questions don't solicit elaborate response, it's clear that the things these children are saying are right at the top of their consciousness. You give them only six minutes and they tell you a great deal. They are the ones that bring up global loss, or the death of innocent people. It's not a researcher or interviewer cleverly manipulating them into saying things that they don't actually hold in their consciousness at all times.

The third question is the hard one: how do we link these findings with the possibility of pathology? This study is an instrument, and perhaps by using this instrument in concert with interview techniques in populations at risk, like adolescents who attempt suicide, we will gain some insight. Perhaps we will see that those children that attempt suicide have a vastly different profile than other children. So, we have begun to get at these three questions, and the answers aren't all back yet, but we're moving forward towards a clearer understanding.

We are still, however, faced with the problem of how to make 64% a meaningful statistic. 64% of a student sample feel that there will be a nuclear war, and 38% state that it will result in the destruction of human kind or other global loss. How do we make people see that this statistic has important implications for the future of these students and for all of us?

FACING THE NUCLEAR THREAT: COMPARISONS OF ADOLESCENTS AND ADULTS

Judith Van Hoorn, Ph.D.

In the story of The Emperor's New Clothes it is the little boy who calls out the naked truth while the adults look on silently. Does the threat of nuclear annihilation present a modern version of this story? The literature on children's responses to the nuclear threat emphasizes their concern. The literature on adults emphasizes their denial of the threat. Are these differences real or illusory? In our cross-age study, Perrin French and I address this question. We examined awareness of and response to the threat of nuclear annihilation across three age groups.

Work in this field generally has been undertaken by scholars looking only at single age categories. They have come from varied perspectives and have focused on different questions. Child psychiatrists and developmental psychologists have asked: "Does the nuclear threat pose a psychological threat to healthy emotional development?" Adult psychiatrists and mental health professionals attempting to explain adult reactions have asked: "Why do adults respond so apathetically?" Social scientists carrying out empirical research on adults have asked: "What are U.S. adults' attitudes toward national policies relating to nuclear weapons and war?" Because the central questions have been framed differently, the conclusions also differ. The literature on children emphasizes their awareness; mental health literature on adults stresses their denial; the politically oriented literature on adults emphasizes that adults agree that there is a threat, yet disagree on the level of risk and the appropriate national response.

In our cross-age comparisons we examined two areas: (1) individuals' assessments of the risk of nuclear war, including both estimations of the likelihood of war and of the severity of its consequences; and (2) individuals' reactions to the risk of nuclear war, including opinions about societal responses -- e.g. military strategy, arms control and civil defense, as well as more personal aspects of response, such as the degree of thought given to the issue, the extent to which individuals discuss their concerns, and actions undertaken as a result of their concern.

Studies of children, predominantly of adolescents, have assessed their opinions about risk and have focused on the personal aspects of response. A large percentage of children in most studies have indicated that they think it is likely that a nuclear war will occur and that they are worried about it (Beardslee and Mack, 1983; Doctor and Goldenring, 1984; Goodman et al., 1983). For example data from the Monitoring the Future Project (Bachman, 1983), a yearly national survey of more than 16,000 high school seniors, indicated that in 1982, 35% agreed that "nuclear or biological annihilation will probably be the fate of all mankind within my lifetime," while 30% indicated "often" worrying about the chance of nuclear war.

Discussion of adults' psychological reactions to the possibility of nuclear war has also centered on risk and personal aspects of response. Here, the focus has been on the apparent apathy of adults in the face of peril. For example, Lifton (1979) has described the psychological response of "psychic numbing." Adults who initially grasp the magnitude of the threat can cease to experience it because of its ongoing nature, invoking mechanisms of suppression and denial.

The theoretical literature on adults (e.g. hypotheses regarding their psychological defense mechanisms) is frequently presented side by side with the empirical studies of children (e.g. survey findings specifying high levels of concern). Both these bodies of literature have been developed by mental health professionals who often present them at the same conferences. This could lead one to the conclusion that children are more concerned than adults. However, the empirical (survey) research on adults, conducted primarily by national pollsters rather than mental health professionals, has rarely been discussed in the same context as the empirical research on children. Comparing the data from studies of children with that from studies of adults, one is initially struck by the similarities in response. The following examples illustrate this. But they also show how difficult it is to make cross-age comparisons using the results from different studies (See Table 1).

We have been unable to find any previous study surveying adolescents and adults simultaneously with the same instrument. Our study bridges the age categories, comparing positions on three focal issues regarding the likelihood of nuclear war, its survivability, and personal response to it.

Participants included 399 high school students, 714 college students, and 126 subjects, 18-81 years old, who were contacted by means of a telephone survey. The total sample size was 1239, 57% female and 43% male. Inclusion of the college students was significant, because while this group has traditionally been the group examined in studies of social movements, it has been a "missing link" in the literature on response to the threat of nuclear war.

We surveyed two areas in Northern California with different ethnic, political, and socioeconomic profiles: the metropolitan San Francisco Bay Area and the agricultural San Joaquin Central Valley. High school students attended four schools: two in the Central Valley commmunity of Stockton and two in the Bay Areacommunity of Palo Alto. College students also attended four schools: Stanford University in Palo Alto, the University of the Pacific in Stockton, California

Table 1

Perceptions of and Reaction to the Threat of Nuclear War

Study/Date	Item	Age	N	Response
1. Estimation of Risk				
a. Likelihood of nuclear war				
Doctor and Goldenring (1984)	Do you think that a nuclear war between the U.S. and the U.S.S.R. will happen during your lifetime?	13-18	913	52.3% yes* 31.9% no
Bachman (1983)	Nuclear annihilation will probably be the fate of all mankind	H.S. Seniors	16,500	35% mostly agree/agree*
Gallup (1983)	How likely do you think we are to get into a nuclear war within 10 years?	Adults	1,504	16% very likely 24% fairly likely 28% fairly un-likely 25% very unlikely 7% no opinion
b. Survivability				
Doctor and Goldenring (1984)	If there were a nuclear war, do you think that you and your family would survive?	13-18	913	64.4% no* 21.7% yes
Gallup (1981)	If we should happen to get into an all out war, what do you think your own chances would be of living through it?	Adult	1,500	32% poor 60% so-so 5% very good 3% no opinion
2. Response				
Doctor and Goldenring (1984)	Have you ever thought about nuclear war?	13-18		33.1% often 57.3% a few times 9.6% never
Bachman (1983)	Of all the problems facing the nation today how often do you think about... the chance of nuclear war?	H.S. Seniors	Approx. 16,500	30% often* 7% never
L.A. Times (1982)	How often do you worry about the possibility of nuclear war	Adults	Approx. 1,500	28% often/a great deal 34% worry seldom 37% worry hardly ever 1% don't know

*other categories not reported

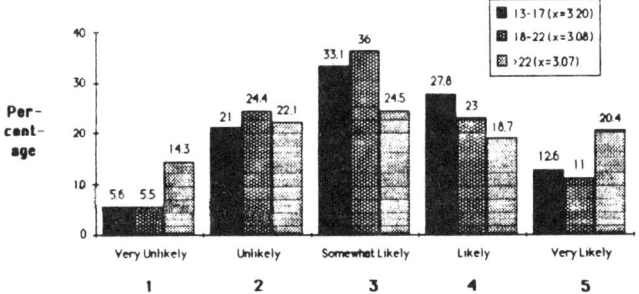

Table 2
LIKELIHOOD OF NUCLEAR WAR BETWEEN U.S. AND U.S.S.R.:
Comparison of Age Groups

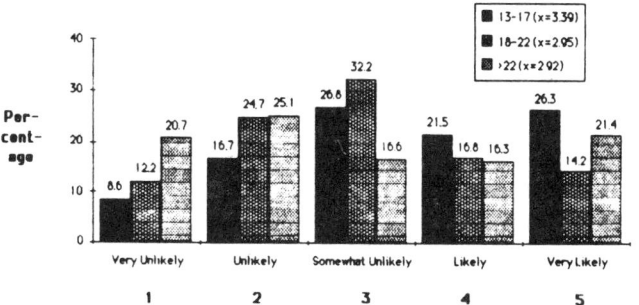

Table 3
LIKELIHOOD OF DYING FROM NUCLEAR WAR:
Comparison of Age Groups

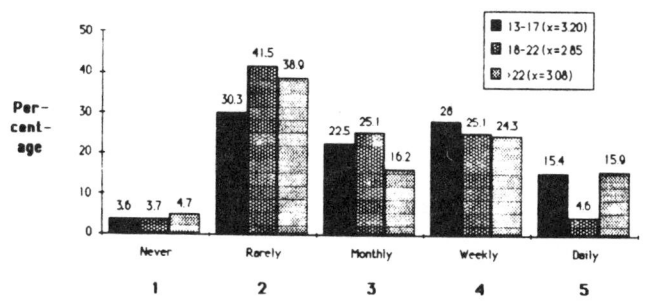

Table 4
FREQUENCY OF THINKING ABOUT NUCLEAR WAR:
Comparison of Age Groups

State College at Stanislaus in Turlock, and San Joaquin Delta Community College in Stockton. The random phone survey was taken in Stockton. The response rate was more than 30%.

The instrument used was the Nuclear War Attitude Survey II (NWASII-Part A), a modification of the NWAS developed by French (see French, 1984a, 1984b for prior reports of its use). It included 27 multiple choice items related to perception of risk and personal reaction. Three items were similar to items in the surveys cited in Table I regarding likelihood of nuclear war, its survivability and the reaction of individuals to its threat. These were:

1) "In the next fifty years, how likely do you think it is that the U.S. will be involved in a nuclear war with the Soviet Union? (Very likely, likely, somewhat likely, unlikely, very unlikely)."
2) "In the next fifty years, how likely do you think it is that you will die from a nuclear blast or its fallout? (very likely, likely, somewhat likely, unlikely, very unlikely)."

and 3) "How often do you think of the possibility of nuclear war? (each day, each week, monthly, rarely, never)."

There are limitations that exist in the sampling procedure. Although information was not collected on socioeconomic status, the San Joaquin Central Valley sample, in contrast to that of the San Francisco Bay Area, included more low income and minority individuals. While high school and college students reflected both geographical areas, all participants older than 22 lived in the Central Valley. The greater percentage of females reflects higher numbers of female students in several of the college classes. Bias in the telephone survey due to self-selection of its participants cannot be ruled out. Additionally, there was a built-in bias in the method of item construction. Five items, whose responses offered a Likert-type scale of 1-5 utilized three "likely" and two "unlikely" categories, yielding a general bias in the "likely" direction which must be allowed for in any consideration of the responses other than comparative ones.

We compared the attitudes and knowledge responses of three groups: 13 to 17-year-olds (high school age), 18-22-year-olds (college age), and those over 22 surveyed in college classes and by telephone (mean age 37). The number of participants in each group were, respectively, 397, 546, 296. The responses to the three focal items are presented in Tables 2-4. Data obtained on all items are presented in Appendices A, B, C.

Age group differences that emerged were as follows:
On the likelihood of Nuclear war:

- Differences among the age groups' responses were not significant regarding likelihood of U.S./U.S.S.R nuclear war, nor for the items regarding the likelihood of a nuclear blast or a nuclear war started by accident (see Appendix B).
- Differences were significant but small for the most generic item, "likelihood of nuclear war." The younger the respondents, the higher the likelihood ascribed to nuclear war.

On the dangerousness of nuclear war:

- Younger people thought it more likely that they would die in a nuclear war (see Appendix B).
- The analysis of other items relating to nuclear war's dangerousness showed few significant differences. Less than 20% of those in any age group expressed the opinion that the U.S. could engage in a nuclear war and keep it limited (see Appendix A).

- There was no significant difference among age groups in the mean number of knowledge items answered correctly.

Personal reaction to the Nuclear Threat:

- Significant age group differences were more consistent among items dealing with personal reaction to the nuclear threat.
- In addition to thinking about the possibility of nuclear war more often, younger subjects were less likely to agree that "there are causes worth fighting a nuclear war for." High school students, college students, and adults came out 10%, 13% and 16% respectively on this item countenancing nuclear war (see Appendix A).
- Although there was a high level of consensus within all groups that nuclear war is preventable, there was a significantly greater degree of pessimism about their own ability to take preventive action among those over 22 years (Appendix A).
- Younger participants were more likely to have confidence in the efficacy of arms control agreements (Appendix A).
- Age group differences were not significant with respect to confidence in effectiveness of civil defense (Appendix B, Appendix C).

Overall age group differences were generally small, even when statistically significant. The greatest difference, on the issue of arms control agreements, was 18% between the youngest (81% supportive of arms control as security-enhancing) and the oldest (63%).

Thus, faced with the same set of questions regarding nuclear war, adolescents and adults in our study were found to respond in similar ways. Significant differences were small and hence of questionable social consequence, but I shall discuss them because of their interest from a lifespan perspective.

The data suggest three age-related patterns. In the first place, adolescents and adults appear similar in their perceptions of the risk of nuclear war but different in their personal reactions to the nuclear threat. When asked about the "likelihood of a nuclear war between the U.S. and the U.S.S.R in the next 50 years, different age groups responded similarly, assigning a likelihood of slightly above "somewhat likely" (the midpoint on a five point scale). In contrast, adolescents reported a significantly greater frequency of thinking about the possibility of nuclear war than adults. Furthermore, younger individuals seemed more likely to think that they could do something about it.

At first glance, the different age group responses to the item "How likely do you think it is that you, yourself, will die from a nuclear blast or fallout?" appear to contradict the proposed pattern of all age groups exhibiting similar risk perception. But though used as a measure of "dangerousness," this item may be seen to combine aspects of "likelihood," "dangerousness," and personal reaction. The questions posed by Gallup (1981) and by Doctor and Goldenring (1984) are cleaner measures of dangerousness per se because they query survivability ("if there were a nuclear war"). (See Table I.) The item on the present survey obliges subjects to simultaneously imagine nuclear war and to imagine their dying from it.

Why do younger adolescents see a higher likelihood of themselves dying from a nuclear war? Does this merely reflect their understanding that with more years of life ahead of them there's a greater probability of nuclear war occurring in their lifetime? The significant difference in estimation of likelihood of death from nuclear war between high school and college students whose life expectancies are only four years apart suggests this is not just the consequence of good probabilistic thinking. Combine this with the finding that the youngest subjects report thinking of nuclear war more often that older subjects and it does begin to look as if the young use less denial, less repression. It could be that younger adolescents are simply more egocentric than adults and would reflect on any issue more in terms of its personal consequences. But the close agreement on other aspects of nuclear war's dangerousness as well as on its likelihood is more suggestive of the conclusion that those 18 and older are actively denying and repressing acknowledgement of the actual and personal consequences of nuclear war.

Why should this be? Part of the answer may be in our other data. Older subjects, albeit a small percentage at most, are more likely to feel there are causes worth fighting a nuclear war for. Perhaps a sense of purpose in regard to nuclear war renders its negative outcome less likely to be dwelled upon. At the same time, older subjects contrast with younger ones in seeing nuclear war as less preventable, with personal efforts of whatever nature and national efforts at arms control less effective in contributing toward its prevention. Faced with a likely holocaust from which one can do nothing to save oneself, and which one believes oneself powerless to prevent, repression and denial must become attractive responses.

A second age-related pattern appeared across all three focal items, and, in each case the standard deviation was greatest for the adult group. The adult group not only exceeds both other groups for percentage of very unconcerned responses (very unlikely/never), it also exceeds both groups for percentage of very concerned responses (very likely/every day). This contradicts the common assumption that the "most concerned" group would have the highest proportion of young people. This difference between the adults and younger groups may reflect environmental differences associated with age. Younger individuals, by virtue of being students, have more homogeneous environments, e.g. similar curricula, textbooks, teachers. Older individuals, not all in schools together, can be more selective in the information they receive -- and tend to select information that supports already held beliefs. This greater heterogeneity in response, however, may simply be reflective of the greater heterogeneity in the group sampled since it was composed of adults 23-83 surveyed in college classes as well as by telephone. We are currently examining cross-decade differences and will be reporting the results shortly.

A third pattern concerns the response of college students, who have traditionally been viewed as being at the forefront of social movements. Based on this stereotype, one might predict that this group would evidence the highest awareness and highest concern. The opposite pattern emerges. This group had the lowest number of responses expressive of concern on all three focal items. In keeping with the overall pattern, the differences were smallest with respect to the likelihood of nuclear war and greatest with respect to "likelihood of dying" and frequency of thinking about the possibility of nuclear war.

The three patterns described above are based on small differences. Moreover, the already noted limitations in the sampling procedure must qualify our analysis. Further studies are needed to confirm the existence of the patterns identified, including studies of the same individuals over time.

Finally, it is important to recall that the similarities among age groups are more striking than the differences. By the time children reach adolescence, their patterns of awareness and response closely parallel those of the adults in their communities. In this, as in other realms of life, children are well enculturated to societal patterns by the time they are adolescents.

APPENDIX A.

PERCENTAGE RESPONDING AFFIRMATIVELY by AGE GROUP

	13 17	18-22	23+	p
6. The U.S. could engage in a nuclear war with the U.S.S.R. and keep it limited in size and location. (True)	12.5	13.5	17.7	.122
7. If arms control talks between the U.S. and the U.S.S.R. had been more successful at earlier times, the security of both nations would now be greater. (True)	81.2	71.5	63.1	.000
8. There are causes worth fighting a nuclear war for. (True)	9.5	12.7	15.8	.046
9. Nuclear war can be prevented. (True)	91.8	91.1	86.5	.045
10. You, yourself, could do something that might aid in the prevention of nuclear war. (True.)	60.0	55.6	46.9	.003

APPENDIX A
(Continued)

PERCENTAGE RESPONDING AFFIRMATIVELY by AGE GROUP

	13-17	18-22	23+	p
Have you expressed your opinions to... (Yes)				
11. family or friends	87.4	84.6	84.7	.385
12. elected officials	6.2	7.6	19.3	.000
13. the news media	20.8	16.5	30.1	.000
Do you intend to express your opinions to... (Yes)				
14. family or friends	87.6	87.8	83.8	.232
15. elected officials	38.7	34.3	45.3	.008
16. the news media	20.8	16.5	30.1	.000

APPENDIX B

MEAN RESPONSE BY AGE GROUP

Item	Age Group			
	13-17	18-22	23+	p

In the next fifty years, how likely do you think it is that...

1. a nuclear blast will occur killing thousands or millions of people?
(1-5, 5 very likely)   3.48   3.36   3.29   .08

2. a nuclear blast will occur?
(1-5, 5 very likely)   3.29   3.15   3.07   .03

3. the U.S. will be involved in a nuclear war with the Soviet Union?
(1-5, 5 very likely)   3.20   3.08   3.07   .21

4. a nuclear war will start by accident?
(1-5, 5 very likely)   2.93   2.78   2.77   .10

APPENDIX B
(Continued)

MEAN RESPONSE BY AGE GROUP

Item	Age Group			p
	13-17	18-22	23+	
5. you will die from a nuclear blast or fallout? (1-5, 5 very likely)	3.39	2.95	2.92	.00
11. how often do you think of the possibility of nuclear war? (1-5, 5 each day)	3.20	2.85	3.08	.00
18. how much should the U.S. Government spend on Civil Defense against nuclear war? (1-3, 3 more than it spends)	1.94	1.95	2.07	.08
Number of factual questions answered correctly.	4.21	4.32	4.35	NS

APPENDIX C

PERCENTAGE RESPONDING ACCURATELY BY AGE GROUP

19. The biggest modern nuclear bombs (25 megatons) are how much more powerful than the one that destroyed the city of Hiroshima? (1800x)

13-17	18-22	23+	p
45.3	42.0	37.1	.19

20. How many nuclear warheads are stockpiled worldwide? (50,000)

13-17	18-22	23+	p
56.6	52.5	53.3	.16

21. Do peaceful nuclear power plants use technology and material from which nuclear weapons can be made? (Yes)

13-17	18-22	23+	p
84.0	87.0	91.5	.05

22. How much of the world's stockpile of nuclear weapons do the United States and the Soviet Union own between them? (99%)

13-17	18-22	23+	p
13.8	12.1	13.9	.69

23. According to President Carter, what percentage of the United States' nuclear forces would it take to effectively destroy most of the Soviet Union's major cities? (1979 figures) (2%)

13-17	18-22	23+	p
33.1	38.5	34.7	.24

24. Would bomb shelters provide meaningful protection in cities hit by a large (several megatons) nuclear bomb? (No)

13-17	18-22	23+	p
89.3	90.2	87.6	.63

25. Two large (20 megatons) nuclear bombs exploded over San Francisco would immediately kill what percentage of the population? (100%)

13-17	18-22	23+	p
57.8	59.9	62.1	.60

26. How many beds are there in hospital burn units in the U.S. capable of providing care for the victims of a nuclear blast? (1,000)

13-17	18-22	23+	p
25.6	30.6	36.3	.03

27. How many U.S. government agencies are devoted to a reversal of the arms race? (1)

13-17	18-22	23+	p
20.1	24.8	30.1	.03

REFERENCES

1. Bachman, J.G. 1983. American high school seniors view the military: 1976-1982. Armed Forces and Society: 10 (1): 86-104.

2. Beardslee, W. & Mack, J. 1982. The impact on children and adolescents of nuclear developments. In Psychosocial Aspects of Nuclear Development, Task Force Report #20, R. Rogers, ed. American Psychiatric Association, Washington, D.C.:64-93

3. Beardslee, W.E. and Mack, J.E. 1983. Adolescents and the threat of nuclear war: The evolution of a perspective. Yale Journal of Biology and Medicine, 56:79-91.

4. Doctor, R.M., & Goldenring, J.M.. 1984. A study of attitudes of adolescents about nuclear war. Unpublished manuscript.

5. French, P. 1984a. The physician as nuclear war educator. New England Journal of Medicine, 310(21): 1397-1398.

6. French, P. 1984b. Preventive medicine for nuclear war. Psychology Today, 18(9): 70.

7. Gallup Report (The), June 1981

8. Gallup Report (The), November 1983

9. Goodman, L.A., Mack, J.E., Beardslee, W.R. and Snow, R.M. 1983. The threat of nuclear war and the nuclear arms race: Adolescent experience and perceptions. Political Psychology, 4(3): 501-530.

10. Lifton, R.J. 1981. In a dark time... in The Final Epidemic. Adams, R. and Cullen, S. ed. Educational Foundation for Nuclear Science, Chicago, Ill.

11. L.A. Times Poll, March 21, 1982.

YOUNG PEOPLE AND THE THREAT OF NUCLEAR WAR IN FINLAND

Tytti Solantaus, M.D.

Dear friends, we have come here from many clinical and research groups, even from different countries, to share our ideas, and work with each other. This is how we make our research true peace research. Research for peace can never be the property of one researcher or one research group and it can never serve nationalistic goals. Research for peace is the property of all nations and all people, no matter where it is done or by whom.

It is well-established by researchers in many countries that young people worry about the threat of war. It is no wonder, because during the years of adolescence many decisions concerning the future have to be made. However, we know very little about the different factors determining the extent of the worry. The aim of our Finnish survey was to chart the extent of the fear of war among young people in Finland. (1,2,3)

The data was collected in February, 1983, by means of a postal questionnaire. This was done as part of a larger study project on young people's health habits. The sample of 12 to 18-year-olds in Finland was derived from the National Population Registry. The response rate was 81%. The questionnaire consisted of 108 questions concerning demographic background, health habits, perceived health and psychosomatic symptoms. The respondents' hopes concerning their own life and future were asked about in one open-ended question with three options, and their fears correspondingly. A subsample of 2167 received eight additional questions dealing directly with peace and war issues. These questions were not given to all respondents, because we wanted to study the hopes and fears without the bias the peace and war questions would induce.

In the open-ended question about fears, fear of war outruled all other fears in every age group. It was referred to by 81% of the respondents. 37% of girls and 15% of boys had experienced strong anxiety about war during the preceding month. A third of the respondents stated that they had discussed peace and war issues at home, about two thirds with their friends. 8% of the respondents thought about the threat of war every day. The threat emerged in the nightmares of every tenth respondent. Just over one third of the respondents were confident in their own ability to contribute to prevention of war.

Differences between boys and girls

Emotional reactions, anxiety and fear were more frequent among girls than boys. Thinking about war was correlated with anxiety more often in the case of girls than of boys. Girls' anxiety level rose slightly though nonsignificantly with age, but the developmental trend for boys was the opposite. Boys expressed more anxiety at 12 than later.

Adolescent girls are more inclined to react with emotions and anxiety than boys of the same age. This is a familiar finding of many studies, and is not specific to issues of peace and war. However, there are certain differences between male and female traditions in our culture regarding war and peace issues, which may explain part of the sex differences.

Men are traditionally socialized to a technological, political and military knowledge of warfare, which gives them the sense of mastery of war, no matter how false this is in the nuclear age. There is no mastery of warfare in women's traditional role. Women's activity during war has not been directed towards warfare, but towards preserving life at home.

Perhaps because of the differences in the two traditions, boys and men are more easily fascinated by the high technology of armaments or the strategic planning of warfare. This tendency is reflected in the popularity among boys and men of computer and video war games. Boys are seduced by the entertainment industry to concentrate on fascinating details of warfare, and this keeps them from seeing the larger context. War games contribute to the compartmentalization and fragmentation of the understanding of war, a theme discussed by Engestroem (4). In this way, war games become part of the militarization process.

Girls, on the other hand, are not so involved in direct militarization. Due to women's traditional role of nurturing, they are in a better position to see the whole social situation of war. Maybe because of this, girls are not so easily enchanted by war games.

Socioeconomic background

There has been some debate on how the socioeconomic status of the family is related to young people's worry about war. It has been argued that concern about war is a problem of privileged youngsters, who have nothing else to worry about. Because our sample was nationwide we had an opportunity to look into this question.

The social classes were defined by occupation: upper white collar, lower white collar, farmers, skilled and unskilled workers. The correlations were not very strong, but an interesting tendency emerged, which was consistent. Concern about the threat of war was greatest in respondents from the first and the fifth social classes. Confidence in prevention followed the same pattern.

These findings can be better understood through the history of the Finnish peace movement. The oldest peace movement began as part of the labor movement and its history dates back to the turn of the century. There have also been peace activists among the intellectuals in the higher social classes all through these years.

Thus, there is a tradition of peace work among both the upper and the lower social classes. Our data did not support the argument that young people from unemployed families and lower social classes in general are not interested in world affairs.

Anxiety about war and confidence in prevention

Peace education is one of the most important areas of education but one of the least developed. We are still debating the very basic question of whether or not it is good for children to study and talk about issues of war and peace.

Our findings suggest that talking with young people about war and peace is an important way to build confidence in their own ability to act to prevent war. Those young people whose teacher and/or parents had talked about these issues had more confidence than others that war could be prevented. Confidence in one's own ability to prevent war is a prerequisite for mastery, through social action, of the debilitating fear of war. Mastery, on the other hand, can be regarded as a criterion for mental health, an important aspect of a socially responsible and competent personality. Schwebel and Schwebel (5) also referred to this as they concluded: "Those who have learnt to cope with the problems by means of personal and social action are more likely to survive unscarred and perhaps to feel more efficacious as they seek to bring about social change."

Our data showed that the young people who were confident of their own ability to contribute to the prevention of war ironically also had more anxiety about war than others. Discussions with parents and teachers evidently support the young in facing up to their anxiety about the threat of war, and in coping with the threat through social action. Those who did not see any possibility for themselves to work towards change reported less anxiety about war and fewer discussions about peace and war issues. They might cope by avoiding the issue, but this was done at the cost of confidence in prevention. This might be part of the process of psychic numbing discussed by Lifton (6), and related to the fatalism discussed by Engestroem (4). These young people are a challenge to health and peace education

Overall, data showed that the threat of war was the most common source of fear among Finnish young people. In fact, Finnish young people expressed more worry about war than Canadians (7) or Californians (8). In a similar open question, 51% of Canadian and 12% of Californian young people referred to war. It is difficult to explain the difference in the level of fear of war, because so few studies have been done on this issue. What follows are hypotheses.

Finland is a neutral country not aligned with NATO or the Warsaw Pact. Finland lives in peace with all her neighbors. Finland imposes no threat on her neighbors and is not threatened by them or any other country. There are no nuclear weapons on Finnish soil, and there is no threat of their installment. This situation might, in fact, be one of the reasons for the high degree of fear of war among the Finnish young.

The psychological situation of Finns is different from that of the citizens of nuclear countries. In the nuclear countries people have to identify both with the role of aggressor and the role of victim. Their own weapons impose a threat to others, whose weapons in turn threaten them. The situation of Finns is more straightforward and simple: we are only victims. I quote Benina Berger Gould because she encapsulated the feelings of many Finns in a comment she made to me. Referring to nuclear weapons she said: "We have ours, they have theirs, but you have them all."

As a neutral country, Finland has no enemies. It might surprise many Westerners to learn that Finland, though a capitalistic country, does not feel threatened by the Soviet Union, our biggest neighbor. This was confirmed by a study (9) among young people, where 85% of the sample stated that Finland had no enemies. 15% did think that Finland had enemies, but no country stood out as being frequently named.

Finland plays no direct part in the actual nuclear arms race, and the citizens of Finland are not as locked into the psychology of deterrence as the citizens of the nuclear countries. This means that Finns are unlikely to trust deterrence policy as a way of preventing war.

The high level of fear of war reflects, on the other hand, young people's awareness of the arms race. This is partly due to the large peace movement in Finland, and also to the active role of the government in peace issues. The peace movement is a grass roots movement in our country. Over 90% of randomly sampled adults (10) support the main focus of the peace movement to establish a nuclear-free zone in Northern Europe -- this is also supported by the government.

The Finnish government supports peace education and peace research. Peace education is an official part of the day care program. In this age group it means teaching nonviolent conflict resolution, and making the children familiar with different cultures through stories and fairy tales. Peace education is now being made part of the grade school curriculum as well. The government has agreed to establish a research unit for studies on the interrelationship of health and war. Later on we hope to be able to host researchers from other countries.

I have gone into some detail about Finland, because one cannot understand our data without some background on the country. The high level of fear among our young people reflects the fact that peace is a major concern in the whole of our society.

REFERENCES

1. Solantaus, T., Rimpele, M., Taipale, V., "The Threat of War in the Minds of 12 to 18-year-olds in Finland." The Lancet 8380: 784-85, 1984.

2. Solantaus, T., Rimpela, M., Rahkonen, O. "Social Epidemiology of the Experiences of the Threat of War among Finnish Youth." Social Science and Medicine 21:145-151, 1985.

3. Solantaus, T., Rimpela, M., Taipale, V., Rahkonen, O. "Young People and the Threat of War: Overview of a National Survey in Finland." In Solantaus, T., Chivian, E., Vartanyan, M., eds: Impact of the Threat of Nuclear War on Children and Adolescents. Proceedings of a Research Symposium. pp 94-103. International Physicians for the Prevention of Nuclear War, Boston, 1985.

4. Engestroem, Y. "Multiple Levels of Nuclear Reality in the Cognition, Fantasy and Activity of School-aged Children." pp 39-52, IPPNW Proceedings, cited above.

5. Schwebel, M., Schwebel, B. "Children's Reactions to the Threat of Nuclear Plant Accidents." American Journal of Orthopsychiatry 51: 260-270, 1981.

6. Lifton, R. J. "Beyond Psychic Numbing: A Call to Awareness." American Journal of Orthopsychiatry 52:619-629, 1982.

7. Sommers, F., Goldberg, S., Levinson, D., Ross, C., LaCombe, S. "Children's Mental Health and the Threat of Nuclear War: a Canadian Pilot Study." In IPPNW Proceedings, cited above.

8. Goldenring, J.M., Doctor, R. "California Adolescents' Concerns about the Threat of Nuclear War." In IPPNW Proceedings, cited above.

9. Whalstrom, R. "Fear of War, Conceptions of War, and Peace Activities: Their Relation to Self-Esteem in Young People." In IPPNW Proceedings, cited above.

10. Johnson, R.N., Pulkkinen, L., Oranen, M., Poijula, S. "Attitudes Concerning Nuclear War in Finland and the United States." Paper presented at the Eastern Psychological Association, Boston, Mass, 1985.

Young People and Social Action

Monsoon Scherr

Corrina Tucker

All photos by Pam Weaver

Maurice Williams

Matt St. John

Gabrielle Nicholson

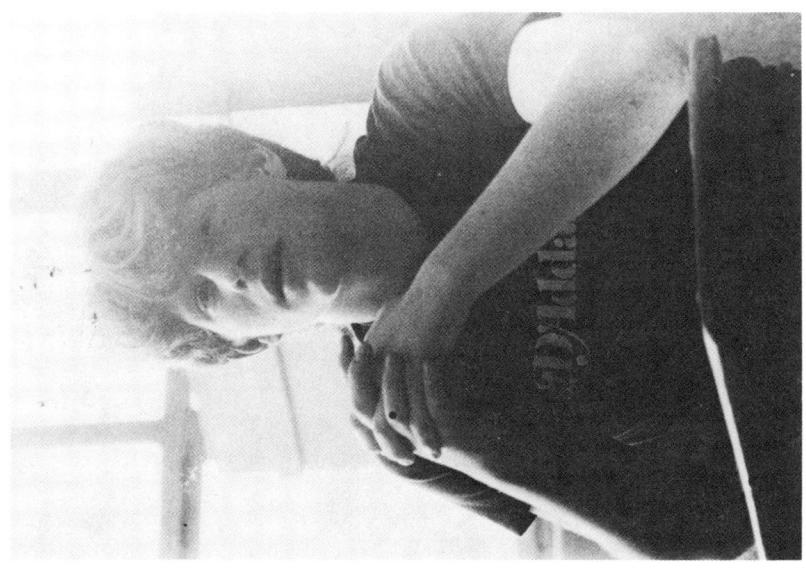

Stefano DeZerega

Jesus Fernandez, Angelic Jones, Maurice Williams, Matthew Weinstein

Gabrielle Nicholson, Wenonah Elms, Jesus Fernandez

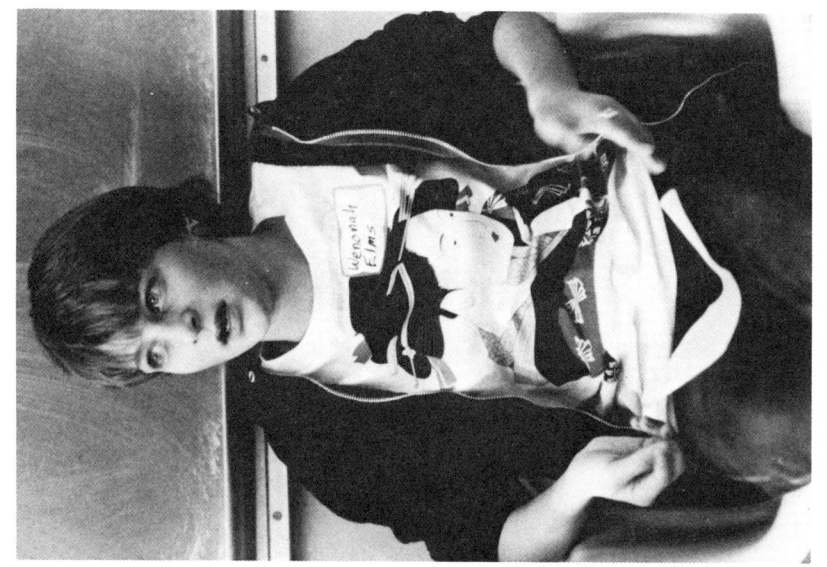

Wenonah Elms

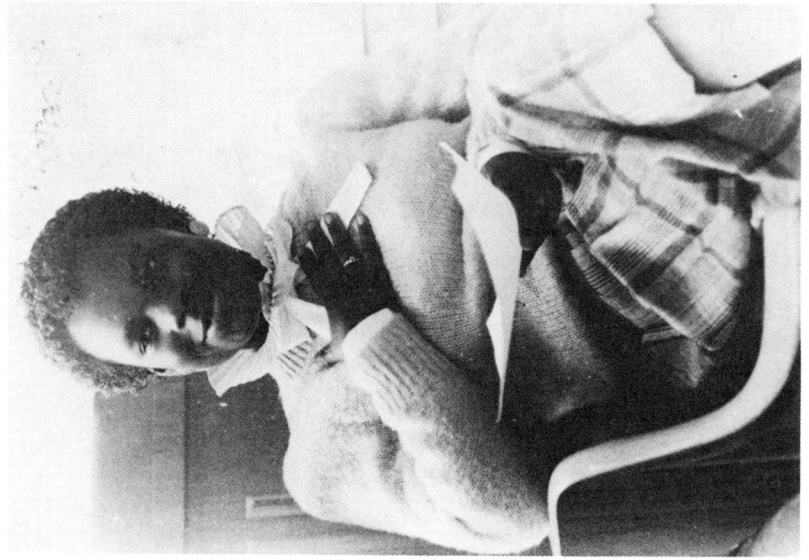

Caila Jones

Angelic Jones

YOUTH EMPOWERMENT FORUM
A PANEL DISCUSSION WITH ELEVEN YOUNG PEOPLE

Benina Berger Gould, Moderator

In response to the need for community dialogue, and to young people's need to be heard by adults, we at the Nuclear Ecology Research Project developed what we call the Youth Empowerment Forum. This model is suitable for school and public settings, and provides an opportunity for sharing of views about our threatened future among different age groups. The forum consists of 8-12 young people, of junior high school and high school age, and a trained adult moderator. The young people sit on a panel before a school or community audience, after hearing a talk by a speaker in this field, or seeing a film on this issue, or both; and as they respond informally to questions from the moderator, they have the opportunity to express their views and feelings about nuclear weapons, social justice, government, the Soviet Union, etc., before an audience of parents and teachers who are really listening to them. After about an hour of panel discussion, the young people usually take fifteen minutes or so to answer questions from the audience, which can be fielded by the moderator.

I have seen this format work well in schools, church groups, mental health settings and town meetings. The participants tend to stimulate and support each other, their confidence grows as they see that they are being taken seriously, and, in my experience, the audience comes away with renewed respect for the sincerity, concern, and understanding of the students.

Benina - First of all, I'd like to thank all of the young people, which is what they told me they prefer to be called, for giving up a Sunday to come out here and be with us as we to devote ourselves to this issue. The young people have been meeting for about 3/4 of an hour by themselves, talking to each other about a set of questions. I'd like to begin by asking all of you to go around and introduce yourselves, tell us what grade you're in, and what school you come from.

Panelists -
My name is Stefano DeZerega, and I attend Berkeley High School. I'm fifteen years old.

My name is Caila Jones. I go to Cathedral High School here in San Francisco and I'm fifteen.

My name is Monsoon Scherr. I'm in seventh grade. I go to Willard Junior High. I'm twelve years old.

My name is Corrina Tucker. I'm a recent graduate of the Oakland Emiliano Zapata Street Academy.

I'm Matt St. John, I go to Berkeley High and I'm fifteen.

My name is Gabrielle Nicholson, I'm fifteen years old and I go to Berkeley High School.

I'm Wenonah Elms. I'm fourteen and I go to Berkeley High.

I'm Jesus Fernandez. I'm a ninth-grader, I'm fifteen. I go to Calvin Simmons Junior High.

My name is Angelic Jones, I'm fourteen years old and I'm in eighth grade and I go to Calvin Simmons Junior High.

My name is Maurice Williams. I'm fifteen years old, ninth grade, Calvin Simmons Junior High.

My name is Matthew Weinstein, I go to Kittredge School, and I'm thirteen.

Benina - Thank you. We often hear what adults have to say about nuclear war, and today we have an opportunity to hear what young people think and feel about nuclear war.

Here is the first question that I'd like to ask all of you. First, please close your eyes. Everybody can do this. Everybody close your eyes and imagine a world without bombs and without the threat of war. Imagine a slide show in your head with the slides flipping by one after the other. Take a moment. What do you see and feel in a world without war?

Matt - When I think about a world without war, I don't see all perfect harmony and love and peace in the sense of no conflict, but I see, if there was no war, there wouldn't be this threat, and always the thought that I might not grow up. But I do see that there would be conflict in the world.

Gabrielle - Well, there would also be a lot more money for other things, social programs and stuff. And just not having it when you're coming home from school, you know and reading the paper or something, not having it there.

Stefano - I see people putting aside their old views of how you deal with conflict. It seems to me the immediate reaction now with a majority of people is to fight it out. If you have differences, you fight it out and whoever's stronger wins. I think that's really backwards. I see a non-violent response to conflict, a different way of dealing with it, a different way of thinking of how people should relate to each other, of how everything should be worked out. I see a world where there is more happiness and there's not as much grief, but it's absence of grief, it's not absence of conflict.

Monsoon - It would be easier to know if you're walking down the street, that you're safe, like just relax at home when you're eating, you know that you'll be eating again tomorrow and the next day without worrying that a bomb might just come down and you won't be eating anymore.

Jesus - When I think about war, it's dumb that it's not doing any good for us and that we don't need it. Instead of spending money on bombs, you should spend it on old folks' homes and giving money to the poor people. What we could do is, we could make a school for the old people, so they could learn and be like teachers instead of being boring. We could give food, so at least they wouldn't be starving, begging for money or stuff like that, you know, and you give money or at least give 'em a chance to like have them learn something.

Caila - And like Jesus was saying that is kind of ironic how the people who make nuclear wars and everything say it's for our good, whereas, like you said, it's taking things away from the majority of the people who really need it, which is us. To me it's not doing any good for anyone, except those, you know, who are making these things.

Jesus - Making money.

Benina - This is a question that's often asked me when I do workshops and meet with parents and teachers and adults. I want to get your opinion. At what age do you think children should be told about war? The possibility of war?

Monsoon - Well, I think that when a kid wants to know what war is about, then someone should tell him, or when he's at that age where he's going to have to vote for it or something he should be told. I don't think you should pressure any kid into having to know. You want to tell your kid, you want to make sure he has knowledge of it, but you don't want to scare him, you don't want to pressure him.

Gabrielle - Kids mature at different times and it's different times for different people. It really depends on when they're ready to deal with it.

Jesus - There's a lot of kids that already know about nuclear bombs and stuff like that and it doesn't matter what size they are or whether they want to know about bombs, it doesn't really matter how big they are.

Benina - You think it doesn't matter?

Wenonah - I think kids, if they watch TV, or have any contact with the outside world, they're going to hear about it and they're not going to understand it, and at a certain age you try to explain it to them, maybe they don't understand, but at least it's a little more help than just hearing the propaganda. I don't think there should be any age bracket. And it's really difficult for a little kid to understand it, but eventually they have to hear about it and it's better to hear about it from someone they know and trust than Suzanne Sommers on the TV.

Benina - You think it would be good to hear it from someone like their parents or someone that they're close to?

Gabrielle - I think it is instilling the values, you know, when the parents and kids talk about it, because that's how values are passed on.

Maurice - I think they should be told only when they hear about it anyway, because it's not like a sport, a team wins and a team loses -- nobody wins.

Matt - I don't even remember when I first heard about nuclear war. But I know now, it's really important to me, to talk to my parents, my friends. So I think basically what everybody was saying, when kids are ready to learn, they're going to want to learn and I think they'll show that.

Benina - How do you know that someone is ready?

Caila - Well, most children, if they want to know, they'll ask questions, you know. Especially, if they're young, like if you wait for your son or your daughter to be our age before, you know, you tell them about nuclear war or just war in general, you know, you're going to have a lot of problems, because, now the generation gap have already started to take a toll of the relationship between your son or daughter.

Gabrielle - People do come to a realization with it at different times in their lives.

Caila - And although our age group might appear that we're just not interested, it's just that we don't really want to talk about it or deal with it. But then some of us feel that it's just a little bit too heavy for our age group.

Benina - I'd like you to think about something. I'd like to ask you, what is your definition of peace?

Caila - Peace comes from a lot of different places. We can't rely on our world leaders, you know, to give us peace. Peace is something that, you know, first you start to get within, then you've got peace with yourself and then you know you can have maybe peace in the home and then peace in the state and peace in the world. You know, it's just something that has to grow from person to person, because, you know, how can any of us begin to make peace where we have a lot of conflicts going on within ourselves, within our families, you know, within our communities.

Stefano - I think that peace is a thing that happens when people treat each other equally. I think when there are some people subjugating others, and trying to dominate them, take advantage of them, use them, it's really impossible to have peace.

Benina - I'd like to hear from everyone.

Corrina - I don't think there is a definition for it. You can't get it out of Webster's Dictionary or whatever. It's got to come within you. Peace can mean a number of different things for everybody. I think that what peace basically means to me is being content, being able to know that someday I will be able to have children and not have to worry about them going to war or bringing them into a world where everybody could be blown off the face of the earth in ten minutes. I think that's what peace is to me, knowing that I have the security, I will be able to have a home of my own, and know that there's no world hunger and know that there's no conflict around.

Gabrielle - Well, my brother once told me that he was never going to have kids because he didn't want to bring them into this world. I think when people start thinking like that, you know there's something wrong -- when he feels that badly about the world he's living in. Peace is a time when he shouldn't have to worry about that.

Matt - To grow up in this day and age is hard enough, just going to school, you worry about doing well, getting along well with people, that's hard enough. So then when you go home and you see a headline or something in the newspaper that's talking about more money that's gone to bombs that are destroying the peace, what I'm saying is that that makes it even harder to live and do well and feel comfortable, when you have these other worries to deal with.

Gabrielle - For me it was really just, it was Thanksgiving morning when I heard that Reagan had, when the U.S. and the Soviet Union were going to have talks. And that sort of made my day a real Thanksgiving, I really felt thankful for something. Even though they're just talking and not going to do a whole lot.

Matthew - My definition of peace would be to think that you can live and have kids and you don't have to worry about being blown up ever. My definition is just not having the bombs at all, just to get rid of them completely, and not have them, that's my definition. No wars going on, because if there was a war going on you would be killed like that. And it's not worth having everybody in the world killed for no reason. I think it's just stupid.

Monsoon - The way to have peace is for people to be trustworthy. Right now a lot of people, it's hard, a lot of people aren't making any money. People take whatever they can. But you have to think about the person next to you and what their situation is, because if you both start fighting over one thing, it won't work out.

Stefano - This is kind of off a little bit. The threat of war, the non-peace that we live in, I think it's really hard, as Matt was saying, to go through with your day. You're at school, you're studying hard, but what am I going to school for, what am I learning all this for if it's not going to mean anything? It's not going to mean anything to me in the future, it's not going to mean anything to the kids I may want to have, it's not going to mean anything to anybody. It's going to be all worthless, it's going to be erased.

Caila - At school we showed a film, Testament, and talking in the hall at lunch, well, what would you do if there was a nuclear war? Most of them said, you know, I would just kill myself, you know, and it's kind of sad that people between the ages of 14 and 16 can say "I'll kill myself" without a second thought.

Jesus - Peace, my definition is like, someone who needed help, help 'em.

Angelic - Did you all see that article in the paper about the budget cuts, cutting welfare and all that? (Laughter) You all know what I'm talking about anyway. Instead of them cutting all that, they could be helping the poor people that's on the street and the ones that live in the parks and are on the street begging for money. You could be helping them with the money that's being spent on the bombs.

Maurice - It's not right to spend the money on the bomb when you've got enough bombs to blow the whole world up three or four times over and it shouldn't be like that, the money should be spent on better things, like old people, to make places for people to stay. Sometimes I feel myself walking down the street and in the air a helicopter and you look in the air thinking of bombs coming down.

Matt - I sometimes feel really fortunate because I've grown up in a society where I've a place to come home to, I have food in my refrigerator, a place to sleep and that makes me feel really good, but it also makes me feel guilty in a way because there's so many other people that don't have that and I feel like I'm betraying them, I mean I feel guilty in a way when I have so much more than a lot of people have. And to relate that to the question, peace would be, the definition of that would be equality and I don't have to feel guilty because I have more than other people do.

Benina - I can't think of anything else. You've said it all in answer to that question. Let's have another slide show. We made a deal. They don't want to close their eyes, and so we made a deal. For one of the questions they'd close their eyes and for the other they wouldn't. So you don't have to close your eyes. But let's have another slide show. Picture a time you felt powerful. If you could feel that power now, what would you do to stop nuclear war? What personal qualities does it take for you to feel powerful? Let me describe some times that you might have felt powerful. Say you were playing soccer and you made a goal. Or let's say there was a time that you were having a discussion with somebody and you were able to use everything that you had to get them to believe something that you wanted them to believe. Or maybe you were just alone, you got up in the morning and you just felt great, felt like you could just take charge. Picture those times in your head. And if you would, share with us a time that you felt powerful, and if you could feel that power now, what would you do to stop nuclear war?

Stefano - I think one of the times I felt most powerful in my life was, I guess, a blockade of Livermore Labs, 1982. And it was an incredible experience. I felt powerful for a lot of reasons. I felt powerful because I was confident in what I was doing, I was resolved, I had some way to get an outlet of my feelings, you know, make a statement. I felt like the group with which I was working was a really neat group, because like we made our own plans, we made our own decisions, and we were all in it together, we were totally equal, and worked by the consensus process and it was just really incredible. And that power didn't last a long time, it really didn't because as soon as we got into Juvenile Hall it was a lot different. (Laughter) But I'll always remember that, I really will. I'll always remember the power that I felt there for a while. I think I can have that power now, I can make that power when I want to. I think there are things that I can do. I don't think blockading the Labs is going to stop the whole issue, it's definitely not, I had no misconceptions that it was when I got into it. But I really think that making those steps are important, to do something for yourself and all the people you come into contact with, all the people you talk to after you get out. I really think the qualities that are necessary for our empowerment are confidence, high self-esteem, equality. Ageism is a serious problem, I think, in this society and I think it's something that needs to be dealt with. And I just think a lot of times parents have a lot of control of how their kids are shaped, because when you're young you're so impressionable. And I think if there's any way you can instill those qualities in your kids and give them that equality that they so deserve, this would be great.

Matt - When I feel most powerful on the nuclear issue, is when I'm taking part in it. At our school, there was just a group formed on the subject of Nicaragua, and so when I take part in groups like that and when I worked for Voting Power and I went around and I went to people's houses and made sure they were going to get to the polls, times like that that I feel powerful. And so although it's so easy to feel helpless, when you feel confident that you're doing something, then you feel powerful.

Monsoon - Sometimes it makes you powerful just going to a demonstration, even though nobody knows you, but you're there and you're helping, fighting for something that you believe in and so that makes you feel powerful, it doesn't matter what anyone else does, you're in that demonstration and you're helping fight just like anybody else. That makes you feel good, and it makes you feel powerful.

Benina - That's very important.

Gabrielle - Well for me, sometimes that makes me feel less powerful because I start thinking, you know, that it's not doing anything. It's not much of an improvement and stuff. So for me being powerful is having control over my own life, because there's no way I can, it seems like there's no way that I can help other people's lives. And my own life is what I deal with.

Caila - And other times, just a simple opinion that you're doing great, a pat on the back, you know, helps me feel powerful.

Benina - That's what I'm hearing -- that there are lots of important and maybe small things we can do for each other, to make all of us feel equal. Anyone else want to add anything to this?

Gabrielle - One thing is, I feel pretty powerful right here because everyone is listening to me and so, you know, it's just one of those times when people are caring about what I'm saying.

Benina - How often do you think about the possibility of war? And if you never think about it, please feel free to say that too.

Corrina - I think of the possibility of war every day. Mostly because what I deal with is peace and justice issues with youth. I go around to different high schools in Oakland and the Bay Area and talk about militarism and the draft and how it affects you. I guess what really got me interested in it was because I have two younger brothers that I've helped raise for the last six years and I don't want to see them going into war. War is something difficult to talk about, especially when you lose somebody. I don't want to have to lose somebody in a war, to have to make people think about it and to make people reach out and do something about it. I think that everybody should sit down and talk about it once in a while. It's hard. A lot of people were lost in a police action, as they call it, in Viet Nam and there are so many other things like the police action in Viet Nam that are going on in the world now and today and so many of our young people that can be taken away to other countries, that they don't really know about. They don't know what's going on over there, they don't know why they're there. Stuff like what happened in Grenada and what's happening in the Middle East and what's happening in Central America. It seems like the United States goes into different countries all the time and they're not helping what's going on here. There's war here in the United States, there's drug wars, there's wars against poverty, there's a lot of stuff that we don't take into consideration and we'd rather go out there for the oil interests or for the uranium for more nuclear weapons and that's not fair. It's not fair for our generation, for future generations or for anybody.

Maurice - I think about war every day. The neighborhood I live in, that's all you hear over there is, "I'll blow you up!" and that's all they talk about so I can't help but thinking about it everyday. I think about it when I go to school, not knowing what's going to happen to me when I'm walking to school.

Gabrielle - I think about it mainly when I come home and, you know, every day there's something in the paper about, about wars going on and it just doesn't affect me as much as it used to because I'm getting used to it being in the papers every day. And, you know, I don't really think about in the course of my day. It will go through my head but I won't just freak out about it.

Benina - There was a time when it was worse?

Gabrielle - Yeah.

Benina - I think we pass back and forth between those times.

Stefano - I think right now for me, I think about war a lot and I think that the reason for that, more than nuclear war or whatever, is the state of the things in Nicaragua for me right now. I know a few people who live in Nicaragua and when I get a letter from them or whatever I can't stop from thinking about the whole situation down there. A friend of mine just returned from Nicaragua on the Witness for Peace. And it's like

I just cannot comprehend the injustice of what's going on down there and at the same time I can't put it out of my mind, because it's like what we hear on the news is reality to these people. This is their reality, these are twenty people who went out to the fields to pick coffee the other day, and they couldn't go and harvest their crops because they were shot down in the fields by the Contras. They were killed, murdered. For me that war, it's so real and so unavoidable that I can't help but think about it.

Benina - Many young people have talked about the idea that we really are at war already. And you can be affected by it even in your neighborhood...

Jesus - I think about war, I mean I, like The Day After when they showed that movie about people being killed, you know bomb over there and people die, well when I saw that movie, I was thinking all night and just suppose they did it, really a bomb shoots, you know, it would be sad and wouldn't do us any good.

Wenonah - The threat of war is sort of always in the back of my mind, everything I do, it's just sort of there. Usually I don't pay any attention, but sometimes it's like I'll get into bed and there'll be a plane going over and I'll think, you know, this is it. Or I'll get into bed and there'll be something strange, there'll be a fight going on in the neighborhood or sometimes the sky is a strange color and it always freaks me out, I figure they just blew North Carolina away and it's coming over, you know. It's not, I don't think about it everyday in the sense that everyday I think it could happen, it's just that everyday it's always there and once a week or so it comes out in a big, I really think about it. Or something happens that makes me just, that triggers it, and I just sit there for an hour or so going, "oh, my god, I can't believe this."

Benina - Do you talk to your parents about these things, about your fears?

Wenonah - Sometimes I want to, but it's hard to talk to my mom, because she doesn't believe that I should have to deal with this. I'm too young to have to deal with this and so when I try to, and so in a way, I don't want her to have to deal with it either. In fact I'm protecting her from it, so you know I talk about facts and what we heard about in school, but real feelings never really come out. It's easier to talk about it with a friend who's my age and is going through the same thing and it's easier to talk about my feelings with a friend who has basically the same feelings than with my mother who's lived through a whole different generation, lived through a different war and has a whole different view of it. I don't want her to have to think about nuclear war any more than I want to think about it so I usually don't talk to her about it.

Caila - I don't speak to my parents about it, but not because I can't. It's just because I feel, you know, like what's the use? This is the one thing that me myself being a fifteen-year-old and another person being two years old and another person being 102 years old, we're all equal in all this, at this point because, you know, it drags everyone down to the same level. And I can imagine myself being a parent. If my daughter came to me saying, "Mom, I'm scared, you know, because I think we're going to have war," and you know it would really hurt me to have to turn around and tell my daughter, "No, I'm sorry, sweetheart, but there's nothing I can do about it." I just feel it's no use.

Gabrielle - I talk to my mom about it a lot and I talk to my dad about it some. But it's just like she knows a lot more about the past histories of things and, you know, things that have led up to an incident or something. So I can always ask her about things and I can always discuss things with her.

Monsoon - I don't talk to my mom a lot, but if there is something I need to know, or even if I'm just feeling a little bit down or something, just about the situation, I can talk to her and she'll lift my spirits. We talk about it, we usually just talk about mostly the positive things about it, not the negative things.

Stefano - I talk with my parents some, and we talk strict politics, we don't get into feelings and that's all right. There's nothing wrong with that. I like to, more like to share my feelings with my peers, whoever, just anybody who's my age who can relate to where I'm coming from, but I don't try to exclude my parents from that, I share with them at certain times, when I need to share with them. And I like, I'll be there for them when they need to share with me.

Benina - The next question is, who do you want to talk to in your family, at your school, or among your friends about nuclear war, and what would you say to them? Who is it that you haven't talked to that you might want to talk to and what would you say?

Caila - Well, at school, well, at my school, we recently formed a social justice awareness club and we've done things like show the movie Testament just to get the people in my school, you know, interested, to tell them, hey, you know, this is going on. And I talk to my teachers and just my friends, you know, to let them know, like to just to say, like if I found out there was a new guy I would go and tell my friends, there's a new guy on the block, I would just tell 'em, so I would say, hey, you know, here's something that's been called to my attention. I feel this is important that you know this. And then after we do that, we'll say, hey, so what are we going to do about it? And we'll just go and do different things like this or the social justice awareness club.

Monsoon - Sometimes it's hard to talk to your friends because some of them aren't aware of it or some of them don't care or some of them are scared to talk about it. So you go up to your friends and you say this or that and they say, so what? or who cares? or something like that and they just turn you down. You want to talk to them, but like I said, they don't understand or something or they just don't want to talk about it. So they just turn you down. So sometimes you don't know who to talk to. You talk to your parents, you might think they won't turn you down. They might answer you but sometimes they might not. Sometimes you don't know who to talk to about it.

Corrina - I think it's important to talk to individuals, because people feel so helpless by theirselves and when you're able to talk to people and in some way let them know that you know what they're going through, you give them some empowerment. That power that we were talking about earlier, you give them that and then you get more and more people to understand about it and care about it and want to go out there and do something and that way you get something done. I mean, of course you're going to feel helpless by yourself. I mean, you know, power is in numbers.

Jesus - That's true what he was saying, if you talk to your friends, they turn you down. I talk to my friends and they cut out. I talk to my friends, you know, about the problems, they just say, I know that. I tell them that I hate violence and he say "Me too." It's kind of hard talking to your friends and so I talk to my cousin, it's easier for me to talk to my cousin, I know him. But some of my friends, they care about it, what's going wrong in the world, what's going on and stuff like that.

Gabrielle - For me a lot of the time, it's like, there's a lot of friends that are just not like that, where you just never talked about it but it's no big thing, you just don't have that kind of relationship. But I have one friend that I can really talk to about things like that. But there's not a whole lot you can say, I mean, you can say, "I don't want to die." "Neither do I," and that's about all you can say.

Caila - And it's not necessarily that hard to find someone to talk to, it's just hard to find somebody who will really take you seriously because I can talk to my friends, they'll say, "Okay, that's great. It's great that you're into nuclear war." But then again they'll turn, they'll turn around and say, "Okay, so what, so what is the social justice awareness club offering you?" you know. It's always like everyone is always searching for an ulterior motive.

Corrina - I think society plays a lot in that because nobody really wants to talk about it, they're scared to talk about it and then the young people see that adults are scared to talk about it so why should they bother talking about it. I mean come straight down to the line, nobody wants to talk about it and that's why nothing's getting done about it.

Benina - Well, this seems to be a great lead on to the last question. Is there anything else you would like to add to the presentation today that you feel would be important knowledge for parents, teachers and friends to know about youth living in the world today?

Stefano - I think one really important thing is that, just to know that we want to do something.

Matt - We just saw a slide show from a friend of ours that just went to Russia. And she was saying that the Russians know a lot more about us than we know about them. I think it would be a lot easier for me if I knew about these kids. I mean in our school they don't even teach Russian. And if they did I think I'd take Russian before I'd take French.

Gabrielle - Well, what I've tried to do is I've tried to have pen pals in different places because I'm really interested in knowing what other people think about America and just how other people live and the differences because I think there are a lot, but there's also lots of things the same.

Caila - First of all I think what would really be important for parents and teachers and everybody else, you know, people our age, would be just to listen. And if you can't understand just <u>try</u> to understand. And second of all, okay, we've been here and we've talked to you, we've established the fact that nuclear war is terrible, we don't want to have anything to do with it, but, you know, even if we got ourselves straight, you know the United States got themselves straight, then you know we did away with nuclear war, who's to say that <u>they</u> would? Who's to say that <u>they</u> wouldn't use their bombs? And here we are, okay, and so if we stop ours, they can still send theirs and we'll still be in the same situation. So I think there needs to be a lot of more talk with them, you know, between the two places, two countries, you know, because even if we did away with ours, who's to say that, you know, we could stop everyone else?

Maurice - I've seen a film of Russia and over 300 pictures from Russia and I don't know why we're having conflicts because it looks the same. If those people were shown to me and I was told that this was part of the United States I would have believed it, because it looks the same as the United States.

Caila - So it's probably like they're thinking we're the horrible, terrible people and we're thinking they're the horrible, terrible people, so therefore nobody's talking.

Monsoon - I don't think an American kid and a Russian kid should have to have problems because the leaders are. Like they have a video hockey game, with the USA against Russia and it seems like it's always like that. And if you have games or anything. "I'll be Russia and you be USA," or something like that. Or USA against another country, it doesn't work out. It doesn't seem like everyone should be fighting or whatever, 'cause like people, like Russian kids and American kids might be friends but just because the leaders aren't communicating right and stuff like that doesn't mean that other people can't communicate, can't be friends. 'Cause some people say, "I hate Russia," and people say, "Why?" Just 'cause our leaders, we're supposed to hate them.

Benina - I thought maybe we could open it up for questions for about fifteen minutes. Anyone else have anything they want to say first?

Stefano - I think it's important to ignore boundaries, because boundaries are meaningless, and build our own bridges people to people, like what's going on, people in the United States trying to help the Nicaraguan people, it's like we're saying, you know, I don't agree with our government, maybe we're trying to change within, but we don't always have to stay within, we can go outside and make our own contacts, our own connections. I think it's important to try to change things in as many different ways as possible, you know. The electoral process is really frustrating, whatever, but it's still one way to try and I think you have to pursue as many different ways as possible.

Gabrielle - It seems to me that a lot of the things that we're brought up with as kids, that we should try to get along with people and diplomacy and stuff aren't applied to life at all in the way you're supposed to deal with people when you grow up. It took me a while to really realize that, you know, I couldn't understand why the two countries were having such problems. It's because they didn't respect each other at all and they just didn't really want to work together for anything. Which, you know, it's totally different from what I've been brought up with and so it just seems really weird to me. And you know, most kids are brought up to share things with people and stuff like that and it's so different.

Audience - One of the things that's come up a lot at this conference is older people are wondering whether there are differences in how kids deal with this issue based on what race they are, whether they're Latino or black or white or Asian for one thing and also whether how you deal with it depends on how much money you have, how rich your family is, you know, how many opportunities you have in the world and stuff like that. And so, I'd like to know from you whether you see any difference in how kids deal with this issue, based on race or the amount of money you have.

Corrina - Can I deal with that first? I think that does play a key role in this kind of issue, the nuclear issue especially. I think that like the women's movement, this issue has been taken mostly by the majority of white society, upper class white. I think that young people that are growing up in the minority sections of East Oakland or San Francisco or wherever, that they think mostly of if they're going to live today because of the drug wars that are on the streets. They don't think so much about a nuclear war, a bomb hitting them. That's what I see with most of the people that I come in contact with. They think about, "Hey, am I going to have food on my table tonight and am I going to be blown away? Is my brother that's out there dealing going to come home? Is he going to be thrown in jail?" I mean, you know, they think mostly of stuff like that rather than this whole nuclear issue because it hits them directly and something like the issue of the whole world being blown up just isn't, just doesn't connect because it doesn't have any reality to them. Now that's mostly what I see.

Monsoon - Well, talking about people who have money or who don't have money, it's like poor people, some people will go out and sell drugs and stuff and other people say, "No I don't want to do that but I need money, but how am I going to get it?" You hear about nuclear bombs and stuff and people say, "That's just another thing to go along with me, because I'm nothing and nuclear bombs are not going to help me. After they go off, it's going to be nothing and I'm already nothing and so why should I try to even help myself?" So a lot of people who are poor, who might have been trying to help themselves, trying to find jobs and stuff, they hear about nuclear bombs and they say, "So maybe I fight for myself, I get a job, I might start to be earning a little bit of money and the nuclear bomb goes off and there's nothing more left so why should I even try to work out my ways?"

Gabrielle - I think it's more cultural differences than actual differences of, you know, having money or what race you are because, you know, the way people deal with their problems is the way they deal with the threat of nuclear war and so, you know, if you hide, if you don't talk about things, you know some families talk things out and really discuss things a lot and you know, other people when they're having problems they just avoid the issue, they'd just rather not talk about it. And so I think that that plays a more major role.

Stefano - I think schools are really valuable because at school you can reach all kinds of different people and when you have things that they can do, ways that they can get involved, I think it helps them to live their own life and not forget about all their problems because they have a lot to deal with. We all have a lot to deal with. It's like you can split up your time. I think nuclear war is one of the hardest issues to deal with because it hasn't really happened yet and although it's effects are already being felt, it's really hard to deal with that when you have so much else to worry about. I think that school is a good place for connections to be made.

Audience - One comment in response to that. As far as I'm concerned, I think it already has happened in terms of Hiroshima and Nagasaki. My question to you all is, I'm wondering how you got involved, how did you get involved in the nuclear issue?

Matthew - Well, my aunt, she asked me if I wanted to be a part of this and so, first she called up and she wanted to talk to my brother, he couldn't come today so I just came instead. She wanted me to talk about nuclear war and stuff, so I said sure and I came today. That's how I got here.

Jesus - I had a teacher, Miss Hirsch, when I was in the seventh grade. I've been with her for three years now and when I met her she was talking, she'd bring in newspaper clippings about war and stuff.

Maurice - She'd tell us to tell what you'd say about war and how you feel about it.

Angelic - I got into when I was in the seventh grade and I first listened to Miss Hirsch and we'd keep on writing and she said, if you don't write, she'd lower our grade. I wanted to get an A in her class, so I wrote. So I started writing and that's how I got into this.

Wenonah - Well, when I was in like the fifth grade, my dad was really involved in The Freeze. Since I was at his house a lot, I learned a lot from him. I didn't do much. I talked about it a little. And then in the seventh grade I joined a group at school and through that I went to the blockade and through that I met Laurie Olsen and worked with the Citizens Policy Center and then went to all this stuff, and she called me a while ago and asked me to come. That's how I got here.

Gabrielle - I basically started to get interested in this stuff from my mom because she's always going through stages of getting worried about things, you know -- fire, earthquake or a nuclear war, so she got freaked out, so I got freaked out, so that's how I first started getting into it. I've always been interested in politics and what's going on in the world but that's how I started getting interested in this issue.

Matt - I think the first time I started getting interested was at King Junior High when Stefano and a friend of his started a group. That's when I got aware that kids were really taking part in this and it made me feel great. And so from then on, I haven't done a lot, but I think what I've done has made me feel good, and Sue talked to me about coming here and I was really happy when I heard about that because I felt like this would be kids saying what they feel instead of a lot of these adults imagining what it's like. I don't know how accurate you were about us, but...

Corrina - I guess I became actively involved with movements and everything a couple of years ago when I started to go to Oakland Street Academy. My teachers there really care and it's first time I've ever had any teachers that really care and they explain to you what it was like, what it was like for them, in the movement during the sixties, and I was always a person who questioned stuff and didn't just take the newspaper as it was or the news as it was and, you know, say hey, that's facts. A lot of times it's not facts. A lot of times it's just something that somebody made up. A lot of times they make a lot of mistakes in the news or whatever. So I've always been one to question, and I guess that's how I got involved because I've got to find out for myself what's really happening out there. And I got, I've been involved with the Citizens Policy Center for about five months now and Laurie Olsen's my supervisor there and she involved me here today.

Monsoon - My mother is real political, and she goes to different demonstrations and stuff and so sometimes she just asks me to go and so I go. First I really didn't understand why I was there. Then I started learning about the different things that were happening and stuff like that and so then I did different things, different people's campaigns, helping them out and stuff.

Caila - Well, just listening to everybody else it sounds like they've been into this thing for years but me, myself, I've only started this year so, compared to them, I'm just a babe. My English teacher, Miss Moore, she started up a social justice awareness club and I joined and I got interested, so I guess I'm really fortunate to have this opportunity to speak freely about my feelings so early.

Stefano - I guess I got involved a few years back basically in being interested in what's going on. I never really knew anything about it. So then I just started to try to inform myself, but I really wasn't into it. Then I was in a play, improvisational theater, and two of the members of that theater were very active in the blockades at Livermore Labs and they were actually coordinating the youth cluster. So I hooked up with them and the next thing I knew, I kind of went in really fast and all of a sudden I found myself on the line there. So that's how I got into it when I first started off, and then I just kept up with it. I guess, I don't know quite how, but somehow I got hooked up with Laurie Olsen, I guess through Wenonah and the other people who worked with her that I knew and so then I got involved with the Youth Peace Fund which I'm on now with Corrina.

Benina - It's time to stop, but I'd just like to add one thing. We have experts all week-end telling us about how young people are affected by the nuclear threat, so it's especially wonderful to hear about it from all of you, in your own words. Thank you.

YOUTH ACTIVISM AND EMPOWERMENT

Laurie Olsen, M.A.T.

I am the Executive Director of the Citizens Policy Center, an organization that exists to encourage the involvement of young people in policy decisions that affect their lives. My Center works with teenagers on issues in their schools and communities -- providing them with the skills and forums to speak out and work with institutions to become more responsive to the needs of youth.

Over the past few years, we have begun to explore issues of empowerment as they relate to young people's concerns about the threat of nuclear war. As the teenagers in our projects began openly expressing fear and anger about the nuclear threat, we became interested in several key issues: if young people are concerned and fearful what do they do with it? Where do they go? And, because our focus is on developing the ability to act, we wanted to experiment with the kinds of support, education and forms teens might need in order to become active in response to their concerns about the nuclear threat.

This work has led us to three major efforts: the first was conducting a summer institute for youth from Northern California who wanted to learn more and to do something about the nuclear threat. In the summer of 1983, that group of teens produced a book called Our Future at Stake, designed to teach other young people about the nuclear arms race and to help them become active. The book has been internationally distributed and the proceeds from its sales have provided the seed funds for our Youth Peace Fund -- a wholly youth-run foundation which provides grants for youth peace activities. All of these efforts have emphasized youth action and responsibility, and much of my talk today will focus on the combined lessons we've pulled from these projects.

I want to talk today about some of my observations from working with young people and to emphasize particularly the very important role of <u>adults</u> -- in responding to and raising issues with youth, in providing resources and approaches to getting information and educating oneself, in helping to find forums and opportunities for action, and in modeling how to live as a hopeful activist in an often frightening world.

Three important threads contributed to shaping our approach to this task. In 1982 we surveyed 320 peace and anti-nuclear organizations in California to find out the extent of youth involvement in the fast-growing grassroots movement. We found that involvement was almost nil. The vast majority of adult peace organizations have no youth members, no youth on the staff, and negligible numbers of young people involved in planning and participating in events. Adults often express concern about reaching out to youth, but the organizations generally reflect a pervasive societal view of young people as passive. "Here is information for teens," "We're going to produce a pamphlet <u>for</u> young people." Children are seen as empty receptacles to be filled up with information, or as blank slates that need to be acted upon. It is not empowering to have something done to or for you. We found that when young people are active on peace issues, it tends to be in their own social groupings -- primarily in school-based groups -- where they plan and meet in relative isolation from the adult movement.

At the time we were doing this research, we became involved in the then fledgling national dialogue about nuclear education. What should be taught? Who should be teaching it? The dialogue at working conferences and with colleagues sharpened our thinking, taught us a great deal, but also honed our view of how our work might be different from what others were doing.

We were not operating in the schools. We did not have to worry about the political realities of what can fly in a school system. Others were doing that. We wanted to look at activism, and activism specifically for those young people who wanted to do something with their fears and anger about living with the nuclear threat. Our role was to educate youth for activism. Our role was to empower.

It has been our observation in working with teenagers that they often become trapped by the contradictions and problems of some peace curricula being used. Information about the nuclear arms race and the effects of nuclear weaponry is being provided, but the curriculum often falls short of providing youth with education about the possibilities and approaches to change. Recognizing the problem, some curricula suggest that students write letters to the President or their representatives in Washington. That is the extent of political education that seems palatable in the schools. But too often, this is far from empowering. Most young people who write letters don't get any response at all, or receive a letter back from President Reagan claiming, "I, too, care about the threat of nuclear weapons and am doing all I can to reduce it. Thank you for sharing your concerns." But young people, ever sensitive to the climate around them, are aware of the tension and the warring attitudes in the international scene. They did what they thought would help. They wrote their letters. Do they feel it made any difference? Do they feel empowered? In most cases, no.

Many of the young people with whom we have worked mention the viewing of a film in school -- <u>The Last Epidemic</u>, or <u>Hiroshima</u> -- as a critical point when their fear increased. They speak eloquently of the feeling of panic that welled up as they walked out of the room, or lay alone in bed that night. Too often education about the nuclear threat does increase awareness but offers little to counteract feelings of helplessness or futility.

Our summer institute on the nuclear arms race was an attempt to provide an experience integrating knowledge with action. It was designed to be education for political involvement. This was -- and still is -- highly controversial.

In assembling groups for our projects, we purposefully select integrated groups of young people, believing that it is important to create groupings that mirror our vision of what we want the world to be. The groups are age diverse -- including the range of teenage years from 12 through 19. The groups are racially integrated, with a majority being youth of color. There is a broad spectrum of knowledge about the issue -- ranging from one young man who could rattle off details about every new missile being planned by the Pentagon to kids who know nothing except that there is "a bomb" and that it might "go off". Finally, we strive to put together groups in which there is a variety of family backgrounds and experience with political activism.

Our summer institutes begin with a two week intensive period (every day -- all day) during which the whole group works together. Then, for six weeks, teams of young people work in internships in peace and antinuclear organizations -- coming together as a whole group on Fridays to process their experiences. This is followed by two weeks at the end of the summer in which everyone works together full time.

We have been unusually lucky to be able to select the group and to be able to work with young people in a sustained comprehensive way. Yet I think that all the observations I am going to make today are applicable to any adult who works with young people -- whether as a parent, teacher, or clinician. I have nine major points.

First, <u>most teenagers do not know that people can and have changed the course of events.</u> When they learn of the nuclear arms race, they feel hopeless because they feel it can't be changed. What we have now will always be. It has nothing to do with their own personal sense of empowerment. They simply don't have a sense that things change or that people have a part in making change. Partially this is a result of how history is taught. In their view, either a great man in a position of power makes a decision and things happen (e.g., slavery ended because Lincoln signed an Emancipation Proclamation) or there is a natural evolution. Another factor is that teenagers have lived a short while, and in their own lifetimes they have seen little change. Therefore, we stress that the current situation is not fixed. We teach history from the perspective of political movements, of people's movements for social change. We teach a history that looks at <u>how</u> people have affected change -- not just the Lincoln with the leadership to sign a proclamation, or Martin Luther King, Jr., but also the thousands who answered phones and stapled brochures and raised funds in the support offices of various movements. We try to give them a sense of the ordinary people in history, of what someone like themselves might have been doing in another era. And we also teach the history of the peace movement and of the non-violence movement.

A second major learning experience we try to provide is <u>contact with adults who are committed to doing what they can to end the arms race.</u> This is important because young people need to know that grown-ups share their concerns, and that grown-ups are neither indifferent nor paralyzed. Many young people voice the belief that, "adults don't care", or "it's up to us, the young people, to do something about it." They feel abandoned by the adult population that seems to have created this horrendous nuclear dilemma and done nothing to stop it. Young people need to know that adults care and are doing something about it.

But there is another reason they need contact with adults who are committed to activism and that is to give them a model of what a life of political commitment looks like. Contact with active adults lets a young person see everything from how a politically aware parent talks to a child about playing with guns, to how a person balances intense political work and urgent meetings with the demands of everyday life. Because many young people don't have contact with politically active adults, and because it is a lifestyle wholly missing in the media, they can't envision for themselves a life of political activity. They need to see and understand how and why anyone would choose a life like that, a life in which material comfort is not a top priority -- to see that it could be an option for them, not just in their youth but throughout their lives.

I've had a lot of teenagers ask me, "Why do you choose to work with kids? How can you work for such low wages?" To choose such a life doesn't make any sense to young people unless they can also see what we get out of it -- the joy it brings us, the sense of integrity we get, the sense of unity with other people, and the feeling of being involved in building a different world. Career counseling and career education in the schools focuses on the student's skills and interests, not on principles, or other things that bring meaning to an adult life. It is our job as activist adults, concerned about the nuclear arms race, to make these issues visible to young people, to help them ask questions about the kind of work they might do and jobs they might take, and to begin to visualize a life style that includes political activism.

There is another important reason for creating opportunities for young people to work side by side with adults who share their concerns. Feeling productive and needed is not a normal experience in the life of an American teen-ager. Feeling part of something larger than oneself and feeling respected by adults is equally rare. We need to build structures in which young people can work side by side with adults in situations in which their contribution is real and matters. A participant in one of our summer institutes, Zaphra, who was 12, said, "The amazing thing is that everyone who works there (Livermore Action Group) is so nice and they are all just volunteering their time because they think it's important. It makes me happy to be there with people who feel like I do about nuclear war. And they really need my help. At first I thought I might not be welcome, but they really needed me!"

Third, <u>we need to help young people develop the activist's survival skill of learning to live with the horror of the threat of nuclear war without being consumed or devastated.</u> Clearly, this is a problem for all of us, but I think there is something about being a teenager that makes it even harder. Adolescents passionately throw themselves into things, and a cause can become their identity, their whole life. Then they crash. There is nothing worse than to see a 17-year-old burned-out cynic who feels he or she has done everything that could possibly be done to stop the arms race, and it didn't work. It is the end of hope.

Part of our job, again, is to help develop a sense of history and of how long things take to change. We need to prepare ourselves for a lifetime of vigilance and involvement on this issue. Nuclear weapons are not going to disappear. We need to learn to live with the threat of nuclear war and, if we are to remain active, we also need to learn to walk away from it sometimes. While the anti-nuclear movement has put a great deal of emphasis on issues of psychic numbing, I have found in working with youth that when they become activists, the problem is not learning to make contact with their feelings of despair and anger, but, on the contrary, it is how to live with them in a balanced way. Over and over I hear from young activists, "How much is enough?" They never feel that what they are doing is enough. Given the magnitude of the problem, and the depth of their fears and anger, what <u>is</u> enough? They need help figuring out when to give themselves permission to stop for a while. A 13-year-old wrote in her journal during the summer institute:

> I try to do everything I can think of to stop the arms race. I think of it all the time. When I'm shopping I pay attention to what

> company's products I buy, to be sure I don't support anyone that makes nuclear weapons. When I ride the bus I spend the time thinking about actions I could plan. This has become my life now. I'm giving my life to this fight to end the arms race. I don't know how I'll be able to focus on my schoolwork, because this just consumes me. There are a lot of plans I have. I plan to get arrested at the next Livermore blockade. But I realize I can't get arrested every time, and I start thinking, "Am I doing enough?" If I don't get arrested at every action, am I inadequate? Civil disobedience feels like the most powerful thing I've ever done. But I keep wondering, how can I keep doing this forever?

This is indicative of the way many teens feel in our summer institute. We found that part of our role as adults was to know when to take a break. We learned, for example, to halt discussions periodically and suggest a boat ride on the lake, or a trip to the movies. We also tried as adults to model with our own lives a balance between our urgent concerns and activities around the nuclear issue and the rest of our lives. We built into our program time to showcase the other aspects of the young peoples' lives that were not related to the anti-nuclear movement.

Fourth, <u>young people need help to develop skills to pursue information.</u> In most schools they're given a textbook or workbook containing all the necessary information or they are taught to look up something in an index and turn to the right page for the answer. But when you are trying to become an informed person in the anti-nuclear movement, much of the information needed is hard to get. Teenagers need to learn that they have a right to information that affects their lives. They have a right to push to get it, and they have a right to insist that someone at the other end of the phone, for example, give them answers. Our approach to teaching about the nuclear arms race included a lot of independent investigation -- and required them to use many different mechanisms for finding information. For example, "What are the civil defense plans for the Bay Area?" Well, they could start with the library and look under Civil Defense and find nothing. They could ask adults, but few would have any idea. 16-year-old Lena started with the yellow pages, and here is what she reports:

> This summer when we tried research about the civil defense plans for the Bay Area, I was really shocked to realize that there isn't really a system at all, and that nobody even knows there isn't a system. I called the number in the phone book first, and I kept getting referred to other departments. I ended up (after 9 calls) talking to the police department that was supposed to handle civil defense. The person who answered didn't even know who in the department was in charge of civil defense, and after a long time on hold I was connected to someone who had a list of shelters, but didn't know which ones were still operational. You see the fallout shelter signs all over town, but there isn't anyone in charge of them. Then it occurred to me to go down to one of the shelters and look for myself. I found that mice had chewed into a box of biscuits. It was pretty grim.

Fifth, <u>teenagers need to be pushed to think about and question what they are hearing.</u> They hear many conflicting opinions about the nuclear arms race and what constitutes "safety." If someone that seems trustworthy or likeable to them says something, they may accept it without really questioning. They are quick to accept a position, too quick, frighteningly quick -- because they want answers. In working with them, we push them hard to pursue information, to question, and to analyze: who is saying something, what their vested interests might be, what their sources are, and whether there might be any reason that person might not want you to know the full truth (whether it is a parent trying to protect a child, or a government agency trying to withhold information). We do this by purposely exposing them to high quality propaganda, reflecting different views. For example, we showed Countdown for America, which is a powerful "peace through strength" film, and followed it with War Without Winners, a compelling argument for curtailing the arms race. Both films use persuasive techniques such as music, ridicule, and innocent children's faces. But it is important for young people to really question why they accept one position over another, what techniques are used to convince them of a position, etc.

Sixth, teenagers need opportunities for activism, and they need adult help in finding and creating them. They don't often have models in their heads for what an individual can do, or how an individual might fit into the process of creating change. They need to know what options there are for action. To begin with, many don't even know about lobbying, rallies, vigils, demonstrations, letter writing campaigns, etc. -- much less have any idea how to become involved with them. Those in our groups who have no political activism in their backgrounds are also very interested in the experiences of those young people who have been involved. For example, Deborah, a 15-year-old, wrote:

> I have never been to a demonstration or anything like that, though I've seen some on TV. I always thought that being involved in anti-nuclear things meant getting arrested, so that kept me away. I'm against getting arrested. But now that I've found that you can go to a demonstration, and that other kids do it, too, and you don't have to get arrested, I think I'd like to do it.

We work to build their vocabulary of actions so when they see a poster for a rally or a vigil, they will know what it is. But there is another point to be made here. Teenagers tend to like certain kinds of actions better than others. They like things that are fun and dramatic and social. Writing letters to the President doesn't seem like fun to them. It's not social, it's not immediate, it doesn't feel like action. In fact, the more active the better. Civil disobedience is a favorite among teens here in the Bay Area. It is theatrical, it is dramatic, it is something that a young person can do relatively easily, it is social, and it feels real -- you are putting your body on the line. But in all choices for action, the social aspect is important because it links them to something larger than themselves --it makes them feel part of something.

> It means a lot to me to be active now. It helps me feel a lot less scared, like I'm not so alone with this fear, that there are lots of other people who feel the same way and are doing something too. I feel safest when I'm with a group of people doing something about the arms race. (Jeanette, 13)

> Working with an organization or going to a demonstration are great because you don't feel alone. And there's such a wonderful feeling of unity with people. You don't know their names, maybe, but you feel they care because you believe in the same things. It's a wonderful feeling. (Wenonah, 13)

As adults, when we try to structure experiences with activism for youth, it is important to think about how to meet the social needs for being part of something, part of a movement, part of a community.

Seventh, <u>teenagers need to develop a sense of personal responsibility, to know that they can have an impact on others and can share what they know.</u>

Adolescence is a time of intense tracking, in many ways -- into sex roles, racially and socially. If you ask a young person to describe the kinds of kids who go to their school, they are definite about labels and about who is in which group: there are the "preppies", the "burn-outs", the "punks", etc. A phenomenon we are seeing now is the emergence of an anti-nuke type on campus. Most often it is a white group, most often it is a slightly hippie or arty group as well. But what happens for all those other students who are also concerned about the nuclear threat? They don't identify socially with the "anti-nuke" group, so they don't feel there is any place to go with their own concerns. It is very difficult to approach a group that is different from you when you are a teenager. In our work with teenagers we emphasize the importance of taking what you know and believe, and sharing it with others -- not just as a philosophy, but as a set of skills. Our view is that each young person should have the skills to become a teacher and an organizer of others. This requires some basic skills, like how to run a film projector, facilitating a meeting, knowing what is involved in working with the media to get coverage for an event, public speaking. It also requires some experience and awareness of group dynamics and a tolerance for other people. Adolescence can be a very judgmental time of life. It is easy to become absorbed in one's own self-image and the desire to be an "insider". Yet an effective organizer needs to reach out to other people, to try to understand who they are. In our own groups we work hard on group dynamics and try to model some approaches to difficult interactions, and techniques for breaking patterns.

Eighth, I want to speak of the <u>courage factor</u> for young people. Speaking out can be very hard to do, particularly if a teenager is unsure of what other people are thinking about an issue. Even wearing a button can seem like a great act of courage. Speaking up in class, or taking a stand publicly, particularly when it may involve adults, is very intimidating to most teens. In our culture there is a pervasive view of young people which assumes they don't know what they are talking about, and is particularly suspicious of political activity on their part. Young people have fears about speaking up in this atmosphere: "Do I really have confidence in what I know and believe? Do I know enough to stick up for my position? Do I dare say what I feel, because then I'm going to have to defend it, and do I know enough to do that?"

Speaking out against prevailing opinion or in an uncertain atmosphere is scary to teenagers. Sometimes they come out with a passionate blurting of their views followed with extreme embarrassment. Other times they may remain silent when they wish they could speak up, and then come down very hard on themselves. In our work with young people we have them role play situations in which they might want to speak up, and we try to help them develop both a sense of humor and a forgiveness for their own difficulties.

Those teenagers whose views differ from their families have a particularly hard time. Their confidence in their own views flags, and they often feel both isolated and not up to the task of trying to share their concerns and information with others. I received this letter from a 15-year-old about two months after our Summer Institute:

> Dear Laurie,
> I hope this letter finds you feeling fine. I'm doing okay except I really miss the group a lot. Yesterday my father bought a package of clam soup that you could store for five years. I asked him why he was buying it and he said to test it in case there was a nuclear war so we could survive on it. It's called Survival Food. Today I noticed there was a whole box of them in the closet. So I asked him what would he cook on if there was a nuclear war, and he said the stove. Now I'm really confused. How can people be so stupid? I thought everything would be probably

destroyed around here and I told him so and he looked at me like I was crazy, and so did my brothers. Arguments like this have been happening a lot in my family now. What I'd like to know is, am I confused or are they confused? I would like for my Mom and Dad to be invited to the December party because I hope you'll be able to educate them a little bit on this matter.

Love,
Regina

Lastly, in addition to all I've said before, I want to speak on the <u>knowledge factor</u>. Young people need understanding of how we got into this nuclear dilemma (historically and politically) and of its real nature. While people often underestimate the sense of danger teens feel, they also overestimate the degree of understanding. There are tremendous misconceptions and gaps in the knowledge young people have about the nuclear threat. I am not speaking of information about amounts of megatonnage. There are some young people we have worked with who hear people talk about "the bomb", and they believe there is just one single bomb. They have no idea which country has it, or how it might go off -- except some also may have an image of a "button" somewhere that will get pushed. Another example is that young people who see many World War II movies on TV and hear about bombs exploding in U.S. embassies don't know the distinction between those bombs and nuclear bombs. The imagery and the language may be there, but the understanding is not. It takes very careful listening on the part of adults to hear the misconceptions.

Perhaps even more important, it makes the nuclear dilemma seem more irrational and unchangeable if one has no sense historically or politically of how we got here. Let me quickly just list the knowledge areas we find particularly important to teach young people:

- what is a nuclear weapon, and how does it differ from weapons in the past?
- concepts of national security (both for the U.S. and the Soviet Union)
- history of the relationship between the two superpowers as a context for understanding why there are tensions and potential conflicts
- how decisions get made and policy formed about the arms race and defense strategy
- the cost of the arms race
- intergovernmental means of preventing war

In conclusion, we as adults need to see our own role in creating a sense of hope and encouragement for young people who are concerned and who want to be active in stopping the arms race. When we are silent, they perceive an adult world in which fears about nuclear war are unmentionable and therefore very threatening. Lack of action on the part of adults seems to them an indication that we've given up on the possibility of a future, or that we don't care. In talking with teenagers we hear over and over what has come to be almost a cliche. They say, "You (the adults) have already had a chance to grow up, but it's our future that you grown-ups are risking -- you don't care as much because you're already at the end of your lives." They say these things with great passion. It is horrifying to realize the extent to which they view adults as being uninterested in the future. They feel abandoned. When we are silent it rings loudly in their ears. When we turn our backs on the nuclear threat, we confirm their sense of abandonment.

> When I think about nuclear war, I just think it's incredible that people would care so little about other people that they could inflict such horror. And if a bomb were being dropped right now I would look around at all

the adults and I would think, "I guess they didn't care enough to stop it."
                    Lena, 16

ADVOCACY WITH TEENAGERS FACING THE NUCLEAR THREAT

Eve Eden, M.S.W.

In light of the research demonstrating that young people are deeply affected by the threat of nuclear war, it is important to question how best to be their advocates as they confront this threat.

Advocacy here implies several things: most basic, to engage in open communication about the issue -- talking and listening carefully to what young people say. Beyond this, it means taking into consideration their best interests, supporting their point of view rather than imposing one's own, and facilitating their efforts toward attaining their goals. My purpose here is to suggest one further element which seems to be of vital importance: to help young people discover concrete action they can take in response to their perception of the nuclear threat.

I will examine this "action orientation" in two ways: first, how it has been employed in several of the existing educational curricula; and second, how I found it useful in a high school workshop I organized in Santa Cruz, California.

Even without a global crisis, adolescence can be a crisis all by itself. The task of forging a self-identity is primary during the teen years. Part of an adolescent's emerging sense of self includes a realistic appraisal of his or her power and influence in the world, and this is hard to know due to a lack of experience combined with the low social status of teenagers, so they continually test the parameters of their power. The result is that they often adopt either an unrealistically grandiose self-image or a pessimistic view of their own usefulness. Sybille Escalona has stated that children's sense of helplessness is reinforced by what they see as the passive response to the threat of nuclear war taken by the adults in their world. As their feelings of helplessness continue, their subsequent inability to face other future problems with a sense of efficacy can be greatly increased. As youth advocates, the pivotal question is: how can we help them expand their self-concept to include feelings of power and authority in dealing with the nuclear issue?

Thus, the cornerstone of advocacy is to help young people with their struggle to feel effective by engaging in meaningful social activities. The question of "what can I do?" should form the basis of any educational program. Certainly, information about the history of the arms race and negotiations, technical data, and the effects of nuclear war are all critical to their understanding. But we want to enable these young people to take in this information and be able to sustain a feeling of potency and power to act.

While the situation I describe sounds rather the same as that of adults, there are important differences which require different interventions. Lifton refers to the process of denial of the threat of nuclear war in adults, or "psychic numbing", in which we live our lives on two planes -- knowing the possibilities yet living day-to-day as though we don't know. Joanna Macy and others have developed effective means of breaking through that denial, by creating an atmosphere where people come together to explore and share their profound feelings of despair and hope. This "despair and empowerment" work has given many people a feeling of greater personal and collective authority in addressing the issue.

The situation for teenagers is different. The collective power of children and teenagers in our culture is objectively minimal. Together in community, they do not tend to feel increased authority. Second, rather than having to fight numbness, adolescents struggle to keep a tight lid on their fears. Their methods are not unfamiliar: seeking comfort and identity in a group, engaging in dangerous or scary situations (fast driving, a diet of horror movies) in order to assume control, and turning to the comfort of parents to provide safety.

Paradoxically, while teens are willing to take certain kinds of risks, they feel inhibited about addressing the "adult issues" of public policy, and require considerable encouragement. This is particularly true at the initial stages.

When developing an action orientation it is important to frame it in the broadest possible context. A good example of this is the U.S. - U.S.S.R. Student Exchange Project in San Francisco, which has developed a curriculum in which American students learn such things as what young people in the Soviet Union think about J.D. Salinger's Holden Caulfield, and they can compare their responses. Through this project, U.S. students correspond with Soviet students, and even travel there, trekking with Soviet teenagers in the Caucasus.

The several existing curricula (The "Day of Dialogue" prepared by ESR, Ground Zero's curriculum, "Crossroads Curriculum for Social Studies, Science and English: prepared by Jobs with Peace) all include activities that are geared toward taking personal action. Writing letters, setting up community referendums, planning a forum at school, writing or performing a skit or play, writing letters to the editor of the school or local papers, distributing pamphlets, volunteering for an organization, designing stickers or buttons or placemats or a world flag, making books for local libraries, composing songs, or holding public hearings were all suggested. A teacher in Santa Cruz had students send audiotapes to one hundred famous people with questions about their views on making peace, from local politicians to movie stars. The students compiled the returned tapes and made a radio program which was aired locally.

In the spring of 1984 I conducted a workshop for 35 9th - 12th graders in Santa Cruz. I came in as a consultant, invited by the principal of the school. These teenagers were particularly disenfranchised, as they had been shuttled back and forth between group homes, and in and out of the juvenile justice system. I was asked to organize a morning-long program with a focus on the threat of nuclear war. Participation in the workshop was voluntary.

The fact that I would be traveling to the Soviet Union in several months provided an opportunity to introduce an action-oriented approach in the workshop. The students agreed to have the session videotaped. I offered to show the tape to students in the U.S.S.R. This was the single most important way of transforming the event from one in which they were simply commiserating with each other into something more potent. Not only did the students form a communication bridge between the United States and the Soviet Union, they also became teachers of American culture. Excitement was generated from the knowledge that other teenagers halfway across the world would be hearing and seeing them.

The morning was divided into several parts: (1) helping the participants identify and express what they were feeling about the issue. This was done in small group discussions, with several students and one faculty member in each group. Drawing self-portraits and describing the drawing was utilized as a technique, as well as sentence completions, i.e., "When I think about nuclear war I feel..."; (2) large group brainstorming sessions focused on problem solving -- what could be done about the issue?; (3) opportunities for the students to share some of their own expertise, i.e., break dancing; (4) individual interviews on videotape detailing their views; (5) writing and reading letters to the Soviet audience.

The solutions they offered for the world's ills indicated some global awareness, that we are part of a world community. "The president of the U.S. should take a peace pledge prior to taking office, " "the world presidents should talk together," or "if we get together, we can do something," were frequently mentioned. The solutions which suggested personal action, however, were more difficult to come by. They felt that there was little they could do to affect a change in the world. Only a few indicated that their hope was related to their own actions or to the actions of people close to them: one girl felt hopeful when she saw people in her own community protesting in the town square; another said she felt good when she wrote a letter to a government official.

One additional note: for many understandable reasons, teachers often feel uncomfortable in dealing with these issues in the classroom. Before even thinking of educating students about nuclear war, time must be taken to work with administration and staff. It is very painful to hear young people talking about their feelings of despair and powerlessness. It is absurd even to imagine that a teacher could present a peace curriculum without support from other teachers, or without training. I recommend a teacher training program, where teachers can become the "students" and explore the parameters of their own emotional and intellectual responses.

Action begets action . Advocacy is the provision of support and direction for young people to act on their own ideas and feelings. They have a great deal to say, and it is crucial that we encourage them to say it.

EDUCATION OR EXHORTATION?
POSTMORTEM ON A "BAD" VIDEOTAPE

Alan and Lotte Marcus

> "I think you're great for having taken the risk of bringing in a tape of something that didn't work...You learn a lot from the bad tapes...I really think it's brave to show your mistakes..."

NOTE: On the last day of the conference, Alan and Lotte Marcus -- writer and psychologist respectively and both long-time anti-nuclear activists -- presented a 20 minute videotape of a teaching they conducted for a class of Seniors at Seaside High School in Monterey in the Spring of 1984. They had come to Seaside in response to an appeal by John Nightingale, an ecology teacher who'd inc'uded -- against some misgivings from school administrators -- the arms race in his survey of threats to the global environment. The videotape could not be shown in its entirety because the firestorm of dissonance it produced used up the allotted time. To the presenters, however, three questions were raised by the event: 1) What was really shown on the videotape? 2) Why did it provoke such a negative response? 3) How does all this fit into the larger context of everyone's concerns for peace?

Alan - To me, the surprising thing was the praise we kept getting for being brave enough to bring in an unsuccessful or "bad" tape. This implied an agreed-upon set of criteria which, apparently, we violated. Only which criteria? What did we do that one ought not to do? How, in other words, did our "bad" tape, say, differ from somebody else's "good" tape?

Lotte - Well, in retrospect, I would've done several things differently at Seaside High. Talked less, and encouraged kids to talk more, for one thing -- something several in the audience picked up on when they accused me of lecturing. But I think what really disturbed people was that we let our opinions and passions hang out so much. There's a big taboo against that. Also, we presumed an authority -- based on our own experiences in the world -- to question some of the things that the students said. I asked the class -- in response to papers handed in complaining of the nuclear threat -- whether they thought nuclear weapons had just appeared one day, in a sort of ballistics immaculate conception, since they didn't seem too curious about how the whole thing had started. And you pointed out, when they complained about having no time for peace activities because of car payments, homework, babysitting, baseball practice, social life etc., that it wasn't a question of time, but only of a reallocation of time. They had time but it was all spoken for. Both those things turned out to be a big no-no.

Alan - Well, let's remember we were not invited to Seaside High as therapists, but as teachers. Sometimes it really seems to me that what Christopher Lasch calls the "therapeutic sensibility" (devoted, in his view, to producing "psychic security" at all costs) is preempting a lot of anti-nuclear teaching territory these days. Whatever else he or she may do, the teacher is supposed to listen and be supportive, while the kids are supposed to vent their feelings and be reassured. And whatever the kids have to say, no matter how simplistic, misinformed, or self-serving, ought to be received respectfully, with non-judgmental attention. We ought to keep in mind, though, that kids sometimes love to tell Authority what they suspect Authority wants to hear -- something I'm reminded of whenever I see delegations of schoolchildren dutifully reciting anti-nuke sentiments before groups of sighing misty-eyed adults. And wasn't it Paul Goodman who warned us that "...the idea of childhood can be stifling, sentimental...used for emotional exploitation of children...and to serve the fantasies of ideologues..."

Lotte - At Seaside High, the students we were trying to reach could hardly be called children, though they <u>did</u> have plenty of accusations to make against the adult world. Most were holding part-time jobs, they came from homes where both parents had to work, often at jobs they either hated or felt trapped in and they constantly worried about such things as car payments, grocery bills, crowded housing, higher education costs, dwindling local job opportunities and so on. They certainly felt far more oppressed by economic problems than a group of aff'uent middle class teenagers would be.

So I think it is nonsense to claim, as some people did, that these things make no difference, nuclear fears touch all youngsters alike, questions of class or socio-economic status don't really figure. We both saw firsthand how the Seaside students' home situation directly affected their inclination and ability to think about public affairs or current events. Their worries about Whether To Trust The Russians or How To Keep From Being Blown Up were always apt to be shoved aside under pressure from the daily nitty gritty.

Alan - Still, they <u>had</u> written a lot about nuclear nightmares in their <u>assigned</u> papers. Are you saying that what they'd written was somehow less real than what they told us in class later?

Lotte - No. I'm saying it was obviously more threatening for them to talk about this in person with us than to deal with it alone on paper. We assumed we could just take up the dialogue where their papers left off. A mistake -- as several pointed out to us. Quoting from their papers turned out to be like quoting from diaries to which they'd confided private, perhaps even unspeakable, secrets. There seemed to be some kind of betrayal involved. And perhaps some of the initial resistance we met came from this mistake.

Alan -   Another mistake, too, was our overestimation of what they already knew. Not just about the arms race, but about the significant events of modern history. We'd been invited to discuss nuclear arms issues with them, yet they had only a dim notion of who Hitler was, couldn't tell us what the Second World War was all about, didn't know how the race for the bomb began, didn't have much sense of the ups and downs of the Cold War.

Lotte -   What stabs me most about the kids at Seaside High is their terrible bleakness of outlook, their underlying resignation. They believe, for instance, that you can't trust politicians ("look at Watergate"); the world's coming to an end ("the Bible says so"); people are always going to fight ("it's just their nature"); what kids say doesn't count ("who listens to kids anyway?"); it's useless to try to change things ("nobody wants to get too involved"); things are going to go smash ("nations are as self-centered as people") etc. etc. Truths, half truths, inherited prophecies and invented myths. And not a helluva lot you can say in reply, either.

Alan -   I recently came across a Peace Manual for educators, with questions for kids conveniently grouped by grade levels, to be asked, as the instructions put it, in an "emotionally neutral tone." ("Where did you first hear about nuclear weapons? Who did you talk to about it? What did it make you feel? How often do you think about it nowadays?") etc. etc. If you have enough patience, the authors say you may help kids discard their feelings of "despair, isolation and powerlessness" and enhance their "confidence, self-respect and self-esteem" as well. But I don't see this as a teaching exercise so much as a kind of upbeat exorcism rite, which describes what goes on at a lot of peace workshops, in-service sessions and anti-nuclear conferences these days.

Lotte - The terrible question, though, remains: no matter what we did, or didn't do, at Seaside High, what can or should we tell the children? I remember the columnist, Ellen Goodman, writing that "children deserve to be heard...deserve to understand we...are working to make this a less scary world..."

Less scary? Okay, how? By engaging in visualization rituals or cutting out paper cranes? Through pen-palsmanship across the seas or hand-holding vigils at missile bases? Does it make things less scary if we scatter peace doves on the Pentagon, or weave friendship quilts to hang beside all the other friendship quilts crowding the dusty cloakrooms in the Palaces of Friendship in the U.S.S.R.? And how about people-to-people contacts multiplying each year while the warheads rise? Does it truly push the doomsday clock back any if we keep sending more peace ambassadors from groups like Bridges to Peace so they can meet for the umpteenth time with Soviet peace committee representatives, and agree yet again -- over soft drink toasts and plates of zakuski -- that 1) war is bad, 2) peace is good, 3) nuclear weapons are awful, 4) people are the same the world over, 5) children are the best ambassadors, etc. etc.? Meanwhile tiptoeing around such unpeaceful subjects as the Refuseniks, Sakharov, the MX, Afghanistan, Solidarity, Star Wars, KOO7, etc.

Alan - Well, the truth is we've both participated in a lot of the stuff you've just mentioned, and will probably go on doing so as long as we are still around. Whether or not it makes things less scary, it certainly makes us less scared of the general scariness, which may be the same thing.

Lotte - The question of what to tell the children, when broached at a PSR conference a while back, called forth rather subdued replies. Erik Erikson advised us to "trust yourself," Professor Craig Schindler of UCSC enjoined us to "speak to that part of the child that is a whole person."

Alan - The question is not so much <u>what</u> to tell the kids as <u>why</u>. What are we doing it for? Are we going into schools to act as lightning rods for their fears? Or to transmit information and stimulate them to direct action? One speaker told us that transmitting information is crucial. Teaching kids the history of the arms race is critical. Yet it must be done in such a way, she said, so as not to diminish their feelings of "potency". We must be careful not to "burden" them too much. And a third accused us of talking "garbage" when we declared to Seaside students that nuclear war is NOT, in our opinion, a viable way to settle disputes. When we do that, it is alleged, we cause those who still think it is to turn off. We lose the chance for dialogue. We sacrifice the proven miracle of the listening cure in which even lifelong hawks, if not argued with but only attended to with steadfast respect, may eventually break down, change their minds, recognize their potential complicity in crimes against humanity. But at Seaside High the students we spoke with were <u>not</u> invalid. The setting was a classroom, not a treatment center. Those anxious about nuclear weapons are healthy, not sick. One has to see the folly of the arms race close up in all its preposterous implausible pathological detail, I think, before one is liable to get indignant enough or mad enough to want to do something about it.

That's what happened at Seaside High. It is exactly what agitated the critics of our "bad" tape. Too much passionate give and take. Too much urgency and anger at the unspeakable impasse those whom Robert Jay Lifton calls the "nuclearists" have gotten us into. But we were lucky; in the event we were able to see some of this urgency and anger rub off on a few youngsters who began to think about taking their own lives and futures back under their own control.

From this point of view -- although we certainly made plenty of mistakes, God knows, -- I don't think our tape can be called all that "bad" after all.

Lotte - I'm wondering if we went back to Seaside High tomorrow, would we be any more effective? And I'm not talking about curriculum, there are lots of good curricula.

Alan - Well, we've already spoken about difficulties the kids seem to have with writing, with language. So we could do worse, perhaps, than try to teach them what language is all about. I remember Jerome Frank lamenting that poverty of language is one of the reasons for the fix we're in. We simply don't have words to name where we are.

Beyond that, there are more fundamental threats to our grasp on reality because of what's happening in our language. A lot of what we've been talking about here has to do with a trancelike use of words to protect and defend us from seeing what we really can't stand to see, to keep us from perceiving what our touch, taste, smell, sight, intuition, tell us is actually so.

As psychologists, for instance, we're accustomed to speak in code. We don't just feel good, we feel good "about ourselves." When we listen to a friend sympathetically, we're "validating" him, etc. As peace educators, we do the same. We talk about teaching kids the arms race in an "emotionally neutral tone" (as if they won't know what we're suppressing and draw their own terrible conclusions). We say we're reinforcing their feelings of "potency and self-esteem" (without acknowledging we may be trying to foster similar feelings in ourselves). All this produces a mountain of verbal sludge, giving off what Robert Penn Warren calls "the authentic stink of artificial language." Meanwhile the situation gets worse, the children get more apathetic or frightened, the language becomes more and more opaque, it becomes more and more difficult for "reality" to sift through.

George Orwell said that sloppy and ready-made thoughts produce sloppy and ready-made phrases, degrading and infantilizing political life. So I think it might be valuable to try to hold up these various self-serving vocabularies -- of hyperbole, doublespeak, euphemism, etc. -- for kids to scrutinize straight on, and try to teach them how to decipher what's being said.

Lotte - Something else we might do, too, is to try to "detoxify" the whole subject with humor. In my experience, peace teaching tends to be a very grim business. And no wonder, with the marvelous bag of goodies (First Strike, MAD, Counter Force, Launch On Warning, etc.) we usually bring with us. But laughter can be wonderful at clearing the air, reducing the whole ghastly panorama to its essential absurdity. We've seen the head of Civil Defense, for instance, telling us that with a handful of dirt and a good shovel, we can "protect" ourselves from radiation! And read of official plans to print "forwarding address" cards, so people in post-attack days will be able to receive their bank statements punctually. And listened to the late Herman Kahn recommending we wear Radiation Meters so if we vomit after an attack we can verify when it's "only an attack of nerves". Children, who have a wonderfully sharp sense of the absurd, ought to be able to respond spontaneously to this sort of macabre -- and perspective-engendering -- humor.

Alan - This is in line with something Freeman Dyson wrote recently deploring the "Eeyore Syndrome." Eeyore is the donkey in Winnie the Pooh who keeps looking at his reflection in a pond, first from one direction, then another, saying, "how pathetic, how pathetic" all the time. That's the precise message given out nowadays, according to Dyson, by too many resigned people contemplating their hopeless future. Dyson wants us to thumb our noses at the "Eeyore Syndrome." He opts for Comedy over Tragedy. The Comic Hero gets into a million scrapes, is nearly done for time after time, but somehow through the use of courage and cunning, and against implausibly long odds, manages to come through. We all have it in us, according to Dyson, to imitate comic heroes whose business is survival, not noble departures, righteous poses, or apocalyptic suicide. We may even, by our example, stimulate others to do the same. And if enough people catch on, who knows, it could even, as Arlo Guthrie once sang, turn "into a movement." That's what I meant when I told the kids at Seaside High that by merely complaining and opting to do nothing, they were, in effect, imitating Eeyore, the Donkey, and at the same time making the Big Bang more likely. Becoming active -- in whatever way they choose -- reduces the odds. Gamble for gamble, there's no question where the advantage lies.

Lotte -   Is that what you think we were up to at Seaside High -- imitating Comic Heroes?

Alan -   Well, I don't recall a lot of belly laughs. But think about it -- two middle-aged peaceniks shaking their pea-sized fists at the outrageously dangerous antics of governments and leaders and generals and daring their young listeners to do the same. It was absurd and inappropriate on the face of it, a scene out of Cervantes. Yet it seems to me if we are to have a chance to save ourselves, or more important, persuade young people that fighting for their world is actually possible, then more such unseemly, absurd, and inapproriate actions might be called for.

Lotte -   Why not? As the song goes, "Send in the clowns." But, clearly, there's no right or wrong way to do this kind of work, this kind of teaching, though there are pretend ways. I guess the burden of what we've been trying to say is: the teacher IS the curriculum! Whatever we do or fail to do, everything we fear or flinch from and yet hope against hope for, all that we <u>are</u>, in sum, is brought, or should be brought, to the classroom. If we try to put a public distance between ourselves and our feelings, we'll soon become ephemeral, indistinct, talking emissaries from the Peace Biz; we'll tend to float right out of the childrens' minds.

Alan - I'd like to send fraternal greetings to other peace teachers, both veterans and new recruits, because I know how hard it is for all of us to hang in for the long haul. Peace movements, as well as Peace Education Efforts, in the past have been notoriously boom or bust affairs. There's so much static and resistance to overcome, of the kind we encountered in our tape, that one can always find lots of reasons to despair. But let me cite in this connection the late Francis Heisler, a distinguished civil rights lawyer, who spent his whole life tilting at impenetrable fortresses, a very practical sort of Quixote who demolished a goodly share of actual windmills. Co-workers used to complain to Francis. They'd say: what's the use, I'm not getting anywhere, no one's listening to me, I don't see how we can win, I'm bone tired, my spouse threatens to divorce me, I'm never home, my friends think I'm crazy, I really can't go on ... Francis' eyes would twinkle. He would listen sympathetically, shaking his head. Then he would nod in sad assent, saying: yes, yes, yes, of course, you're absolutely right, it's terrible, disheartening, things look pretty grim right now, plenty of good reasons to quit, I don't blame you for getting discouraged. But nevertheless, <u>do it anyway!</u> With Freeman Dyson, we ought to thumb our noses at the spectacle of Eeyore, the donkey, shrinking from his own image in the pond. But with Francis Heisler, we ought to laugh in the face of woeful precedents, current alarums, and dire prophecies, spit over our left shoulder for luck, and keep on "doing it anyway". Amen!

Workshop Summaries

EDITOR'S NOTE ON WORKSHOP SUMMARIES:

On each day of the conference, small groups met in informal workshops, to discuss public policy, community mental health, or clinical psychotherapy, in relation to the nuclear threat. Conference participants chose to attend whichever workshop was of interest to them. We asked each team of workshop facilitators to write a summary of their workshop, making use of the taped transcript where one was available. (The workshop on public policy was not taped.)

We include these informal summaries here because we think they are useful examples of group dialogue. Such workshops as these provide an important opportunity for active participation and processing of new information for people, who, in a more passive mode, have been listening to speakers' presentations. Furthermore, the material itself suggests a number of creative approaches to the problems discussed.

THE NUCLEAR THREAT IN THE CLINICAL HOUR

Ellen Becker, M.F.C.C., and Barbara Green, L.C.S.W.

Our working group consisted of 30 psychotherapists interested in examining the relationship between psychotherapy and socio-political issues. These clinicians represented a broad range of therapeutic methodology and geographical regions, and served diversified economic and class populations. Two of the questions raised became identifiable topics for discussion:

"How, as clinicians, can we evaluate and understand the impact of the nuclear threat on the psyches of our clients?"

"Is this an appropriate area of exploration in the clinical hour?"

Why is it so difficult for the therapist to respond when references are made to the nuclear issue, and why are the inhibitions so strong against identifying the client's feelings about the nuclear issue? Several participants acknowledged that their clients had spontaneously referred to the threat of nuclear war as one of their life concerns, but because the therapists themselves did not know how to respond to these references, they simply ignored them, and instead addressed more traditional therapeutic concerns. One participant expressed his personal fears about the nuclear peril and recognized that he would have difficulty facilitating client exploration while he was still defending himself against exploring his own fears. As this dicussion proceeded, there was general agreement that, as with other areas of therapeutic concern, therapists had to have confronted their own feelings in order to effectively help their clients to explore the issue.

"I was in a gestalt training group and doing a piece of work. I was feeling a lot of anger about our planetary crisis. Finally I heard myself saying, "We're so stupid, we're so stupid, we're going to destroy ourselves!" And some of the other trainees in the group said, 'Come on now, you can't be that upset at the world situation -- it's got to be something else.' I felt invalidated."

Another therapist reported her client as saying, "I've started therapy, because working as a peace activist has brought up a lot of stuff -- some people think I'm really crazy to be scared, and I'm accused of being obsessed about this. So when I decided to go into therapy, I knew I would have to find a counselor who was involved with doing peace work."

Many therapists who had indeed been working with their own personal fears of nuclear annihilation still had questions about what kinds of interventions to make with clients, when to intervene at all, and when to simply listen. Essentially, they posed the question, "What do we have to offer as clinicians, once we acknowledge our clients' concerns?" A child therapist wondered whether you should suggest steps toward action. "Let's say a 16-year-old brings up the fear of nuclear war in therapy. Do you at that point say, 'Look, you could work on stopping this; this is what you could do.'"

Several family therapists indicated that references to the nuclear issue were more likely in sessions where children or adolescents were present. A participant gave the following example: "A family with an adolescent son is leaving therapy for a two-week vacation, and the therapist says, 'Well, I'll see you in two weeks.' The kid, a rebellious teenager, who hasn't said much in therapy for a month, answers, 'How do you know you're going to see me in two weeks? I mean, the world may blow up first.'" This therapist later acknowledged the client's fear as real, and was open to further exploration of how his fear impacted on his daily life.

However, another participant cautioned, "I wonder if the issue came up as hyperbole, as an expression of frustration, a dirty dig at the therapist and parents. Maybe his referring to war was like a curse word, like saying, 'Fuck you!'and had nothing to do with nuclear fear."

The group was particularly surprised to hear other therapists give accounts of children as young as preschoolers making reference to their nuclear fears. And one therapist commented, "Perhaps the nuclear threat should be looked at as a family violence issue. Perhaps the violence and the threat of violence in the world create more violence in the family."

After hearing from the larger community at the conference and from family and child therapists, most workshop participants agreed that children of all ages and various backgrounds are becoming increasingly aware of the nuclear threat. Although most therapists felt that the arms race and its ramifications had become legitimate therapeutic concerns, on both the metaphorical level and on the level of external social reality, some clinicians continued to question strongly whether the nuclear issue had a place in psychotherapy. One said, "When I was separating from my parents, politics was the vehicle I used. It wasn't that it didn't have any validity, but it certainly was what I used to get my own identity, separate from theirs. I think of that motivation with some of the clients I have now who are very political and are also going through a process of separation and individuation."

When the workshop reconvened for a second meeting, clinicians presented specific examples of the ways in which their concerns were reflected in their work. "There are points in therapy where it becomes clear to me that the only thing that's going to be deeply meaningful for a client is to do something for his or her fellow human beings, some kind of service. I saw a successful businessman in his late thirties who talked about his conflicts with his children, wife and employees, but I kept hearing that a piece of himself was unfulfilled because there was no service commitment in his life. The nuclear issue could come up in that context as one of a number of ways people might look at the world and find some way to make a contribution."

References were made to play therapy and the use of toy guns and soldiers as intrapsychic representatives of aggression and violence. We acknowledged the importance of interpreting the play at an intrapsychic level, as well as validating the real threat experienced by children. We agreed that it was important to examine our own countertransferential feelings, to look at each case individually, and to avoid making general pronouncements about therapeutic interventions concerning the nuclear threat.

In conclusion, workshop participants recommended that all gatherings of mental health workers should include on their agenda the psychological aspect of the nuclear threat. As one participant commented, "It might be that the definition of mental health has to be broader now. You know, Freud's was -- the ability to love and to work, and now maybe there's a third area, which is the ability to make a planetary commitment."

COMMUNITY MENTAL HEALTH AND THE NUCLEAR THREAT

Howard Hamburger, M.F.C.C., and Deborah Weinstein, M.F.C.C.

The workshop on community mental health and the nuclear threat included eight people, most of whom were physicians. Our discussion focused on ways to communicate with people who disagree with us about how to deal with the nuclear threat. How do we engage others, even those with radically different perspectives?

The group agreed that it is important to work within our own communities, so that projects reflect the needs of the community and come from the community itself. We don't wish to be perceived as outsiders forcing our ideas upon the community and stirring up children's fears.

It is important to find the common threads between ourselves and people of apparently opposite belief. This requires us to truly listen to a person with a different belief about nuclear deterrence. Do we take the risk of being tolerant, or do we go for the short-term benefit, and block out that person's concerns in order to argue against the deterrence mentality? If we allow ourselves to listen, we create the possibility of being changed, as well as the possibility of changing the other person. It might be that a survivalist has something to offer us.

A common thread that does connect most of us, regardless of whether we are "hawks" or "doves", is our concern for our children. It is helpful to stay focused on this commonality when talking to others. Even if deterrence policy is successfully preventing nuclear war, it is also taking a toll on children. Keeping ourselves and the other person focused on this can help take the discussion beyond political rhetoric to our common concerns.

We also considered the strategy of trying to reach those people who are uncommitted, rather than trying to convince those who have already made up their minds. This would mean that rather than debating, we would express our own beliefs, sincerely and in different ways, in the hope of reaching our target population.

Many of these issues became concrete when one of the participants, a pediatrician, said she wanted to talk to the principal of her daughter's high school in an effort to create programs in the school to help students deal with their feelings about the nuclear threat, but that she was very anxious about whether she would be able to communicate with him on this controversial subject. At this point we did some role playing, in which the pediatrician played herself, and another workshop participant played the part of the school principal. Other participants gave feedback to the role players. We hope the following excerpts from our taped session are both entertaining and helpful.

Dr. A. - I've come to talk to you today because there's something that I'm interested in that I think would be valuable for the school to look into -- a presentation, probably first to the parents and then to the girls, looking into the issue of how the girls can become more informed and more able to have an impact in the world today.

Principal - What kind of thing did you have in mind?

Dr. A. - Well, specifically, I have some knowledge about how children in this age group are anxious and fearful because they don't understand world affairs. I'd like to present some activities to them that would increase their knowledge and give them a way to deal with their anxiety.

Principal - That's very admirable. You know in our Social Studies class we really cover that, and that's the kind of thing we're already doing. Even though it's a very controversial thing, we've given a lot of thought to it, because we don't want to arouse more fears. I think if you ask your daughter, who's taking the class, she'll tell you that these are the kind of things we're already doing, in keeping with the traditions of the school.

Dr. A. - I agree with you that we wouldn't want to stir up any more fear. That would be a mistake. And specifically, we'd like to do it in a way that won't offend people. It's an issue that's known to be of widespread concern, and we'd like to talk about it on a feeling level.

Principal - Well, you know, I've been to the Board about this, and they really feel that this is the kind of stuff that should go on in the home and in the church. We're trying to prepare your daughter and her classmates for college. I'm sure that you have a big influence on her, and this is the kind of thing that's really appropriate for you to do. Our job is to educate your daughter so that she can get into the best possible college.

Dr. A. - (To participants) He's being very nice, he's being a brick wall, and I'm up against my unwillingness to be a little more pushy. My life history is that I got where I am by being pleasant and accomodating. I don't have much experience with getting pushy, especially when someone is empowered to deny me.

Leader - Just for the hell of it, be pushy. Just go to the absolute extreme. Could you get into that?

Dr. A. - I could get into that. (To Principal) You're just another redneck in a perfect Ivy League suit, you know. Here are these girls, they need this information, and you and all these weird parents with their heads stuck in the ground don't want to let them know about it. And they already do know about it, and you assholes contribute to the thing that keeps it all going. No wonder the world is so fucked up.

Principal - I can see you're really concerned about this. (Laughter) You're really cute when you're angry. (Laughter)

Leader - (To Dr. A.) Even though your words weren't wise, strategically, I noticed the aliveness. All of a sudden you were sincere, you were really there.

Participant - This guy's the principal of a school, he must have a soft underbelly, something that hooks him in. Find the right spot and then use your enthusiasm.

Principal - One of the things that made it easy for me is that you're just being a mother. As far as being a respected physician or anything, well, you have yet to show me anything about who you are.

Leader - In other words, you have to pull rank. Go in and say, "Hey, I have a specialty in this area. I know something about health, especially about children's health."

Participant - I think you should start over, and come in with a whole different attitude.

Leader - About who you are.

Participant - Following that other dumpy lady that came before. (Laughter)

(The role play begins again)

Principal - Hello, nice to see you. Why don't you have a seat? You have a wonderful daughter -- she's doing so well. What can I do for you today?

Dr. A. - You know, of course, that I'm Beverly's mother. I don't know whether you also know that I'm a pediatrician in town, and one of my special interests in pediatrics has to do with adolescents, and how they are dealing with the anxieties that are raised by the current state of world affairs. I've spent the last couple of months going to conferences and learning a lot more about this, because this area is a special interest of mine, and I'm enthusiastic about sharing some ideas which I think would be valuable for the school, the parents and the girls.

Principal - You know, I'm concerned about this business, too, but I'm not sure it would apply to our girls.

Dr. A. - Why not?

Principal - Well, I've heard that this is not a real concern so much as something that a lot of people have stirred up.

Dr. A. - I think a lot of people wish that were true. But there's a lot of good data now, that really proves, with good methodology, that the fear is pervasive, and cuts across the socio-economic spectrum. These kids really want to see the issue dealt with.

Principal - The Board's discussed our specific responsibility concerning this issue, and we feel that this is really the kind of thing that should be dealt with at home and in church.

Dr. A. - I'd love a chance to address the board, because if they could know what I know, I believe they'd feel differently about it.

Principal - Well, the Board may be willing to hear you make your proposal, but they aren't going to meet for a couple of months. I'll be speaking with them in the early spring, and I'll bring the matter up for you. I think that's very appropriate.

Dr. A. - I'm glad you're interested. I'd be happy to go along with you to the Board meeting. What, specifically, do I have to do to get on the agenda?

Principal - Well, I'll get back to you on that. I'll speak to the President and I'll get back to you.

Dr. A. - The President sets the agenda?

Principal - Well, yes, ordinarily. I'll speak with him and see if we can get something going.

Dr. A. - That's very nice of you. Between now and then, maybe I could float you some information, so you'll know specifically what I'm talking about, and I'll get back to you in a couple of weeks to see what's happening with the agenda.

Principal - That's fine.

Dr. A. - Unless you're going to be out of town, of course.

Principal - No, no. (Laughter) No, I'll be in town. Has Beverly spoken about this?

Dr. A. - Beverly speaks about this only once in a while, in a way that I think is pretty average. She's not having nightmares or anything. She's currently a lot more scared of the biology teacher.

Principal - Why don't I get the school records and see how's she doing -

Dr. A. - It's nice of you to offer, but I don't think Beverly's schoolwork is really the issue. I think it's a pervasive problem. I don't believe Beverly is especially troubled. We know from some of the studies that kids from families where the parents openly discuss the nuclear threat have more of a handle on it. Many of your girls may come from families where it's not really talked about openly, and it's not that we want to open a can of worms, it's just that you're trying to educate girls to be competent and to make some impact on the world, and this is a specific area where we can really do something to make them become the kind of people that you would like them to be.

Principal - Well, actually, I've been thinking about the same thing. You know I think it's about time that one of the things the school does is to take a more active interest in this area. My wife and I are really very sympathetic to this point of view. What I'm worried about is the Board, and other parents. You know, this is the kind of thing that can upset parents. It can give the school the reputation for being a place for rabble-rousers. As much as I support your idea, we don't want that kind of reputation. What we do want is for our girls to be able to go to good colleges. Our more conservative parents, and some of the Trustees, whom we really depend on for their generous gifts every year, could take offense at something like this, even though you and I know it's really very important.

Dr. A. - I can see that that would really concern you, because obviously the school depends on that money to keep going. Perhaps what I should do, as you and I are working to make this happen, is, in my role as a pediatrician and a member of the larger community, to talk to one or two of the people that might be the most influential in this area, just on a one-to-one basis, and see if we can't start things in the direction we want them to go without stirring anybody up.

Principal - Tell me more about what it is you're going to want to do.

Dr. A. - Well, specifically, I want to provide the opportunity for them to be open with their thoughts on the issue, to share their ideas about world problems, and what the solutions might be. We certainly don't want to channel them into accepting someone else's political definition of the right solution. Our goal is to educate them and empower them, not to indoctrinate them. If you and I talk to the Board about this, we have to make that very clear.

Principal - This is the kind of thing that goes on at home all the time. I'd say my children, for example, feel really free to discuss these things with me. These are things we talk about all the time around the dinner table, the threat of war and that kind of thing. As I said before, I can't help wondering whether there's any advantage to having the school address the issue. What you're talking about is the kind of thing good parents do all the time.

Dr. A. - All children aren't fortunate enough to grow up in a family where that kind of discussion happens. You know, there's data on children not being open with their parents about their fears because they're protecting their parents. They don't want to worry them.

Principal - I don't want you to take this the wrong way, but are you having trouble communicating with Beverly?

Dr. A. - I want to reaffirm to you, I'm not worried about Beverly. The nuclear threat is a problem for every kid in the country, and two thirds of them are scared about it.

Leader - Let's stop the role play now.

In the ensuing discussion of the role play, the participant who played the part of the school principal made some useful comments. He said, "I couldn't get you with the easy stuff, couldn't deflect you. And I got nervous when you said you were going to meet with my bosses. So I tried to suck you in, to get you a little worried about what you're doing, you're rabble-rousing, and that kind of stuff...

"You really didn't package it in a way in which I could buy it. I needed a clear plan of what this thing was going to look like, and how it might be fun and helpful for the students. For instance, you could have said, 'In Piedmont,, there was a wonderful forum in which twelve high school kids talked to adults from the community about world affairs, and about their hopes for changing things through the democratic process. This is the kind of thing I'm talking about, because our children learn all kinds of good ideas in this school, but they don't get the chance to talk with adults who are really listening. As a pediatrician, I feel it's terribly important to give our youth, who are so bright and sensitive, a chance to be heard.' Then I could say to myself that I know our students -- I don't see any rabble rousers, and this crazy woman isn't going to stir them up. They're not going to embarrass me...

"All I wanted was to avoid embarrassment. It would have come as a great comfort to me if you had brought me a concrete study with concrete results. I needed to know that I wasn't going to make a fool of myself in front of the Board or the parents."

The role-playing underlined the importance of being clear and focused, prepared with appropriate information, self-assured, and yet sympathetic to the other's concerns, particularly in order to find ways to make it safe for the other person to go along with you, even a little way.

We ended this workshop by stating what each of us had learned and what action we hoped to take as a result of this learning. Our pediatrician was excited about scheduling an appointment with the school principal.

The participants were struck by the effectiveness of the kind of support group we had just been a part of, and some who didn't already belong to such a group hoped to return home to create one for themselves.

AFFECTING PUBLIC POLICY

Eve Eden, M.S.W., and Wendy Roberts, M.S.W.

In order to understand how we, as helping professionals, can influence public policy, we must have at least a rudimentary understanding of what public policy is and how it is shaped.

Some of the questions we considered in the workshop on public policy were: Where does U.S. public policy originate, what are the steps it goes through in the process of being accepted or rejected, what is the role of public support, and what are the intervention points along the way? Where is our best opportunity for leverage, as mental health workers and educators?

It is noteworthy that the workshop did not focus on the possibility of creating public policy, but only on intervening in its formation and process, especially through the channel of influencing public opinion. It certainly seems to be easier for those of us dealing in human psychology to imagine influencing the general public's attitudes than to imagine directly influencing or creating legislation. While this may be the best use for our particular talents and skills, it puts us in a reactive position vis-a-vis public policy. And as there is in recent history a sad lack of correlation between public sentiment and legislative policy, it is unclear exactly what the effect of public opinion is on public policy (public policy being defined as policy that affects the public, but is not necessarily shaped by or in response to a public need or demand).

We reached consensus that there are three basic ways for us to impact policy:

1. by affecting the general social climate surrounding an issue, i.e., using the media to change public sentiment,

2. by affecting legislation, especially with regard to votes on appropriations,

3. by affecting policy makers personally.

As to the second point above, Richard Smoke walked us through the funding of a weapons system, from initial research to deployment, taking the Trident D5 warhead as an example. He underlined the importance of intervening as early as possible after a weapons system is in the pipeline, mentioning the following intervention points: Congressional vote on money for research and development, creation of a Project Office in the Pentagon for a particular weapons system, and Congressional vote on money for production.

We felt most at home with our ability to affect public policy indirectly by mobilizing public sentiment, through the dissemination of information about the psychological consequences of living in a precariously balanced world.

To do this effectively, we would have to make an impact in the media, with credibility and legitimacy, as was done by Sagan et al with the "nuclear winter" findings. Using Sagan's model, we discussed the idea of joint research on the psychological effects of the nuclear threat on children and adolescents in collaboration with social scientists in the Soviet Union. Should the findings be significant, they could be released at a major international conference, held in Sweden or Finland or another neutral country. If this was handled correctly and the research methods were impeccable, the publicizing of these findings could force the governments to respond.

Another possible action would be the convening of a national or international young people's symposium on the subject of the nuclear threat, which would bring young people together to interact with each other and with the media, and would afford policymakers an opportunity to hear what children and adolescents are saying. Such a symposium could be sponsored by groups like NEA, PTA, NASW, and APA.

We acknowledged the importance of learning to use the media effectively, and two of the suggestions made in this regard were to set up teenage talk shows, and local cable shows, in which local concerns about peace and the nuclear threat are discussed.

Other ideas generated during brainstorming were:

- Develop internships for kids, where they can learn about influencing policy

- Influence policy makers' children

- Support AB 38-48 (California Assembly Bill allocating money for the study of and ultimate creation of educational curricula on the nuclear issue)

- Have public state and federal hearings on the issue, including young people with varying points of view as participants

- Organize teachers' unions to take a stand

- Encourage education about Soviet life, in U.S. schools

- Introduce a bill to subsidize Russian language education

- Write articles

- Develop curriculum for a Peace Academy on how to teach foreign policy in high schools

- Research what makes people feel empowered

- Help kids go on strike till policy changes!

Participants in the workshop were people who work primarily in the fields of psychology and education. We were not a group of politicians, and public policy was a subject we all faced with some degree of trepidation. Most of us work actively for peace, and yet, in regard to public policy making, we tend to feel the terrible sense of helplessness so frequently associated with the nuclear threat.

We considered the way in which PSR (Physicians for Social Responsibility) has used the expertise of its members to create a national awareness that nuclear war is medically contraindicated, and we talked about how we could use our own expertise in human psychology and child development to focus attention on the fact that the nuclear arms race is psychologically contraindicated. Our discussion underlined the importance of educating ourselves about public policy-making, trusting in our own knowledge and experience, and speaking out whenever we could find both the courage and the opportunity.

Conclusion

CONCLUSION

Susan Moon

During a recent trip to the Soviet Union, I visited a grade school in Leningrad. At the end of a seventh grade English class, the teacher urged her students to practive their English by asking questions of their American visitors. A small boy in thick glasses stood up and asked shyly but with great intensity, "Do children in America struggle for peace, like we do? I was glad to be able to tell him that many American children, my own included, work hard for peace, by marching, demonstrating, writing letters, talking on the radio, and otherwise expressing their concerns to those around them. I promised him that I'd tell children in America about his question.

When I came home, I didn't think about this Russian boy until I went to a school in El Cerrito, California, to talk to a group of seventh and eighth graders about my trip to the U.S.S.R. After I showed some slides, I asked if there were any questions. They sat quiet a moment, blinking after the darkness, until a tall black girl asked, "Do kids in Russia want peace as much as we do?" Then I remembered to keep my promise to the boy in Leningrad.

The title of this book poses a question - "growing up scared?" This question has recently become the subject of increasing controversy, in a time of backlash against the nuclear freeze movement. Robert Coles writes that only a few very privileged children are afraid of nuclear war (New York Times Magazine, 12/8/85). Joseph Adelson and Chester Finn claim that the only frightened children are those who, too young to understand about government themselves, have been "exploited" and "terrorized" by political activists (Commentary, April, 1985). But the answer that comes out of this book is -- yes, too many children are growing up scared.

Three researchers here describe their respective studies, each of which found a high degree of worry about nuclear war on the part of the respondents. Jeffrey Gould, whose study found that 64% of the subjects think there will be a nuclear war, suggests that research should turn to the question of how the nuclear threat relates to young people's preparation for the future and to pathologies such as teenage drug abuse and suicide. Judith Van Hoorn sees the need for further study of adults, in order to better understand the process by which concerned young children sometimes become unconcerned young adults. Tytti Solantaus describes the Finnish government study in which 80% of the respondents expressed a fear of war, this fear outruling all other fears, in Finland, a neutral country with no nuclear weapons.

Researchers agree that they have not been able to do much more that scratch the surface. We can't claim to have all the figures. We don't know the exact number of frightened children, or the percentage of nuclear nightmares. But we do know that many kids are scared -- too many -- and we don't need to be able to quantify that fear precisely, before we can say, with one of the youth panelists, "Hey! We know this is going on -- Hey! So what are we going to do about it?"

The twin concerns of Growing Up Scared? are how to help children grow up whole and hopeful in a threatened world, and how to publicize the psychological damage being done by the arms race. Richard Smoke points up the fact that deterrence policy is based on a system of thought which ignores the psychological implications of that policy for the very populations who are both "protected" and threatened by it. He urges us to call the attention of policy makers to our psychological insecurity, to our children's insecurity. Those who plan for our national security through nuclear weapons need to know that their system isn't working in the most literal sense, because it makes so many of us feel more insecure. The damage done to our children's sense of security is one more compelling reason for disarmament.

All of us who are concerned about young people and who work for peace, in whatever way, must squarely face the charge that our children are scared because we, their well-meaning but misguided parents, teachers and counselors, have frightened them with unnecessary and inappropriate knowledge, and with our anxiety. I believe it's important for us to recognize the portion of truth in this charge. When the youth panelists were asked how they got involved in the issue, one girl replied, "I basically got interested in this stuff from my mom. She got freaked out so I got freaked out."

While we recognize our responsibility in bringing before our children frightening issues, we must remember that the information is out there, too. We didn't make it up. They get it from the media, and from their peers. More importantly, the dangers are real, whether we speak of them aloud or not, and they must be faced if we are to survive.

The dangers are indeed horrible to contemplate. No wonder, as John Mack tells us, parents and therapists have a great resistance to recognizing the social reality which contributes to children's nuclear fear, preferring instead to see such fears as individual, phobic, even pathological, but able to be cured by a good doctor. Nevertheless, Mack's 12-year-old client easily makes the distinction between her "reasonable" fear of nuclear war, and her "unreasonable" fears of ghosts and monsters. Furthermore, children appear to be as likely to protect their parents from the dreaded subject as the reverse. One of the youth panelists comments, "It's hard to talk to my mom, because she doesn't believe that I should have to deal with this...In a way, I don't want her to have to deal with it either. In fact, I'm protecting her from it, so you know I talk about facts, and what we've heard about in school, but real feelings never come out." Perhaps our children have more strength than we give them credit for.

It's painful to pull our heads out of the sand. But this is only the first move. Ron Lally says we must, for our survival, educate our children to a new understanding of the interconnectedness of all life, by teaching such things as nonviolent conflict resolution and appreciation for cultures other than our own. Eve Eden speaks of the importance of helping teenagers to feel effective by engaging them in meaningful social activities, like making a videotape of themselves to send to Russian teenagers. Laurie Olsen stresses that young people's anxiety is reduced when they take positive action for peace. If we give them information about the arms race, we should, at the same time, help them find ways to work against it. Olsen gives examples of some of the social change activities which the teenagers she's worked with have thrown themselves into wholeheartedly, and from which they have gained a sense of community, of hope for their future. According to Tytti Solantaus' study in Finland, children who reported that they talked with parents or teachers about nuclear war were more likely to express anxiety about nuclear war than those who did not discuss it, but they were also more likely to express confidence in their ability to help prevent nuclear war. Expressed anxiety correlates with optimism.

If we teach Russian in our schools, some will study with interest, eager to cross the barrier of language. If we and our children join together with friends to write letters, or participate in a pecae march, or send school supplies to Central America, our children will gain a sense of community, and they will see that their time and effort is valuable to that community.

Unless we want the next generation to leave the world exactly as they find it, exactly as we have arranged it, we need to raise and educate our children to be responsible members of society, with the courage and resources for making change. They need to be activists, in the broadest sense. As Alan and Lotte

Marcus say, it is is not comfortable, for us or our children, to face the issues that must be faced, but comfort is not the point. The Marcuses urge us to reveal our own passionate concern to young people. We can't seek a complacent comfort for our own children, at the same time hoping that somebody else's children will do the dirty work.

Not only is the arms race damaging the world's children with fear, it is also starving them to death with its lopsided economy and choking them to death with its poisons. Many children around the world are growing up with more immediate fears that the fear of nuclear war: hunger, illness, unemployment, drug wars, family violence, bombs falling on their villages. We need to learn as much as we can about how the conditions that give rise to these fears, too, are connected to the arms race, the cold war, and the military economy.

Our fears are fed by our many boundaries, boundaries we erect between ourselves and our enemies. A youth panelist says, "I think it's important to ignore boundaries. Boundaries are meaningless." Let's save our contempt, not for the "enemy", but for the boundaries, visible and invisible, that separate us: the moats, the barbed wire, the trade embargoes, the iron curtains and the concrete walls. I don't say these boundaries are not real, but we have made them real by our systematic belief in them, and we believe in them together, in a joint effort with our so-called enemies. What connections can we make real, then, if we believe in them together?

This is not just philosophizing. There are lots of places to begin the work of making connections, and there is work already begun which must be continued. Some examples relevant to children would be: a joint U.S.-U.S.S.R. research project on how children cope with the nuclear threat; student and cultural exchange programs with the Soviet Union, and other "enemy" countries.

The contributors to this book are asking us to look for ways to help children feel connected, to gain the self-confidence and the sense of responsibility, albeit heavy, that they will need, in order to change the priorities of our society, and to find the joy that comes from doing what needs to be done.

Appendix: A Review of the Literature

CHILDREN, ADOLESCENTS AND THE THREAT OF NUCLEAR WAR: AN INTERNATIONAL PERSPECTIVE

Monika M. Eisenbud, M.D., Judith L. Van Hoorn, Ph.D., Benina Berger Gould, M.S.W.

As a result of public focus on today's nuclear realities, adults and children in countries around the world are increasingly aware of the meaning of nuclear weapons, and the possibility that nuclear war could occur in their lifetime. Survey studies of American and Swedish adults indicate that the expectation of nuclear war has become widespread in those countries (1,2,3) and that most adults believe that nuclear war cannot be survived. The question has been raised as to how widespread children's and adolescents' awareness and concern is about nuclear weapons, both in countries which possess nuclear weapons and in those which do not. Attention is beginning to be focussed on possible short-term and long-term consequences for children who are growing up in the climate of fear and uncertainty about the future produced by the nuclear arms race.

Research addressing these questions was first undertaken in 1961, but has been carried out mainly in the last eight years, and so far has concerned itself primarily with the adolescent age range. The first studies are American, but since 1983, the attitudes of youth are being explored in an increasing number of nations. Comparisons of international data have just begun. This paper reviews the studies conducted to date, summarizes current understanding about the effects on children and youth of fearing nuclear war, and considers approaches for promoting psychological health in children growing up with the threat of nuclear war.

1. Studies conducted in the United States, from 1945 to the present.

Schwebel, 1961 and 1962 (4): Schwebel's research, the first to consider what effects the threat of nuclear war might have on the psychological development of children, was prompted by the international tension that followed the building of the Berlin wall. It was a time when "fear was rife in the nation, and people were engaged in a debate on the adequacy of deterrent force and of fallout shelters as solutions." "But what of the children?", he went on to ask. "Were they a special breed inured to crisis because they had to live their entire lives in the shadow of the thermonuclear mushrooms?" To determine their reaction to the crisis of this period, Schwebel conducted a questionnaire study of 3000 junior and high school students from a variety of backgrounds in New York, Pennsylvania, and New Jersey. They were asked to respond to three questions: "Do I think there is going to be a war?" "Do I care?" and "What do I think of fallout shelters?" In the 1961 study, 45% of junior high school students and 42% of senior high school students replied that they expected war. Students from all age groups and geographic areas expressed concern. In the 1962 study, carried out after resolution of the serious Cuban missile crisis, 23% of students expected war. Based on this finding, Schwebel hypothesized that increased stress can increase denial.

Escalona, 1962 (5): The purpose of Escalona's study was to determine how students viewed the future. The sample included 311 children aged 10-17 in the New York City area, representing widely different socioeconomic backgrounds. In an effort to minimize bias that might be introduced by questions that were explicitly about war, she chose open-ended questions such as: "Think about the world as it may be about ten years from now. What are some of the ways in which it may be different?"

The startling finding was that 70% of the children spontaneously mentioned issues relating to war.

Beardslee and Mack, 1978-1980 (6): As members of the American Psychiatric Association's "Task Force on Nuclear Developments", Beardslee and Mack engaged in an exploratory study of adolescents' responses to nuclear developments after they discovered a sixteen-year absence of research in this area. They surveyed 1151 high school students from cities in Massachusetts, California and Maryland. Questions included:

"What does the word nuclear bring to mind?"
"How old were you when you first became aware of nuclear advances?"
"Have you participated in any activities related to nuclear technology?"
"Have nuclear advances influenced your plans for marriage, having children, or other plans for the future?"
"Have nuclear advances affected your way of thinking about the future, your view of the world, and time?"

The responses to these questions indicated a great deal of awareness, often from an early age, and revealed substantial concern. Answers were filled with vivid and disturbing images of the devastation nuclear weapons could cause. Beardslee and Mack concluded that "thoughts of nuclear annihilation had penetrated deeply into the consciousness of children and adolescents." Students expressed unease about the future, and many were fearful about the possibility of nuclear war. They doubted that it could be limited, and didn't expect to survive if it occurred. Seventy percent felt that their country would not be able to survive a nuclear war. In 1983, Goodman and Snow collaborated with these researchers in an interview study of 31 Boston area high school students from various socio-economic backgrounds, to further explore adolescents' reaction to the nuclear threat. (7)

The results expanded on the findings from the questionnaire studies. Students expressed fear, sadness, and feelings of helplessness about the prospect of a future threatened by nuclear war, and responded with anger to adults' seeming lack of concern.

Goldenring and Doctor, 1983 (8): These investigators conducted a study to compare students' worry about nuclear war with other traditional concerns. Their study design has become the basis for several of the studies conducted in other countries. They administered questionnaires to 913 students in grades 7 - 12 (age range 11-19) in two major California cities. The sample was drawn from lower-middle to middle income families, with above average educational level. The ethnic distribution was broad and representative of the area studied. After supplying demographic data, students were asked to spontaneously list their three greatest worries, in answer to an open-ended question. Then they were asked to study a list of 20 worry items (where "nuclear war" was listed eighth), and rate each (1 = not worried, and 4 = very worried). Their next task was to choose their five greatest worries from this list, and rank-order them. To minimize bias, twelve specific questions about nuclear war were put last in the questionnaire. Results: Three greatest worries: 7% spontaneously named "nuclear war", and another 5% mentioned "war". Among the list of 20 worries, "death of parents" received the highest rating: 74.4% rated it either 3 or 4 (mean 3.16). "Bad grades" was next highest (mean 2.95) and "nuclear war" was third (mean 2.69). In students' ranking of their greatest five worries, from the list of twenty, "nuclear war" received the second-highest ranking, after "parent dying".

Multiple choice response to nine out of the twelve questions that dealt exclusively with nuclear issues are summarized below:

1. How old do you think you were when you first heard about nuclear weapons? 51%, age 5 to 10; 41%, age 11-13.

2. Have you ever thought about nuclear war? 33% often; 57% sometimes; 10% never.

3. Have you talked to your parents about nuclear war? 51% not at all; 39% a few times; 10% often.

4. Do you think that nuclear war between the U.S. and Russia will happen during your lifetime? 9% definitely; 42% probably; 32% probably not, or definitely not.

5. If there were a nuclear war, do you think that you and your family would survive? 64% no; 22% yes.

6. If there were a nuclear war, do you think that the U.S. would survive? 51% no; 36% yes.

7. Do you think nuclear war between the U.S. and Russia can be prevented? 77% definitely or probably; 11% probably not; 4% definitely not.

8. Thinking about nuclear war has affected my plans for the future. 24% yes; 68% no.

9. The amount of information I have received about nuclear war in school is: "not enough" selected by 42%. In a subsample, 44% considered themselves very or somewhat uninformed, and only 10%, very well informed.)

Other findings from Goldenring and Doctor's study are that the students more worried about nuclear war had better scores with respect to adjustment and self-esteem, talked more with their parents, and were more hopeful than the less worried students that nuclear war could be prevented.

Bachman, 1975 to 1984 (10): This ongoing national study entitled the "Monitoring the Future Project" has the aim of surveying the lifestyles and values of youth and young adults, with special focus on drug-related issues. Three items deal directly or indirectly with nuclear war. The fact that this study surveys a national representative sample of adolescents sets it apart from all the other American studies to date that assess attitudes about nuclear war. Groups of high school seniors were surveyed in successive years from 1975 through 1984, with sample sizes for the different years ranging from 16,662 to 18,924.

The questions related to nuclear war asked about students' expectation of "global annihilation", their expectations of a "major world upheaval", and the frequency with which they worried about nuclear war. The latter item was included among questions about a number of national problems. Results: Students' concern about nuclear war showed a steady rise from 1975 to 1982, with those worrying often increasing nearly four-fold (from 8% to 30%). The study results from 1983 and 1984 show that concern has essentially remained at the higher of these levels. Those who stated that they have never worried about nuclear war decreased steadily between 1975 and 1982, from 23% to 6%. Students who agreed, or mostly agreed, with the statement that "this country will be caught up in a major world upheaval in the next ten years" increased from 36% in 1975, to 45% in 1982 (37% in 1984). In the years between 1975 and 1982, those agreeing, or mostly agreeing, with the statement that "nuclear or biological annihilation will probably be the fate of all mankind within my lifetime" increased from 22% to 36% and dropped to 29% in 1984.

Gould, Berger Gould, and Eden, 1983 (11): This study was based on the three questions used by Schwebel in his 1961 study (see above) and was conducted after the Soviet downing of a Korean airliner. The study group of 256 ninth graders from 3 cities in California and one city in Maine, (a subsample of the larger sample of 1700 young people) represented a wide range of socioeconomic backgrounds and intellectual achievement. In response to the question "Is there going to be a nuclear war?", 64% answered yes, while in Schwebel's 1961 study, 44% of respondents answered "yes" to the question, "Is there going to be a war". As in the 1961 study, students indicated substantial concern about the war risk, expecting massive destruction if nuclear war occurred.

Van Hoorn and French, 1983 (12): In a research project designed to include an age group underrepresented in earlier studies, these investigators included older adolescents and young adults in their survey of attitudes and knowledge about nuclear war. The study group consisted of 405 high school students, 721 college students (most 18-22 years old), and 158 additional subjects over age 18 who were contacted through a random phone survey. The sample was drawn from two areas in northern California whose ethnic, socioeconomic, and political profiles differed. Results: A large majority of subjects from all age groups considered nuclear war at least "somewhat likely." Only 14% of the total sample replied that nuclear war between the U.S. and the U.S.S.R. could remain limited. As to the frequency of thinking about nuclear war, 11% replied "daily"; 25%, "weekly"; 21% "monthly"; 37%, "rarely"; and 4%, "never". The youngest subjects (high school students) thought about the possibility of nuclear war most often, and the college age students least often.

Those who thought about the possibility of nuclear war more often also considered it more likely, yet frequency of thinking about the possibility of nuclear war was positively correlated with the belief that one could personally help to prevent it. For example, 67% of those aged 13 to 17 who thought about the issue daily believed that they could help prevent nuclear war, while only 28% of those who claimed never to think about the issue thought they could personally help prevent nuclear war. There was a positive correlation between expressing opinions about nuclear war to family and friends, and the belief that personal action can help prevent nuclear war. Compared to the other age groups, the 18-22 year old college population responded least often that nuclear war is very likely, and reported thinking about nuclear war less often than all the other age groups.

The following information regarding work with young children and families is included here because although exploratory and less formal than the previous research cited, these are informative approaches to important new areas.

Family Studies: Studies of the way in which families respond to the nuclear threat are still in their earliest stages. Two investigators, Zeitlin (13) and Rudin (14) are among those who have made beginnings in this new area.

Zeitlin applied his clinical experience as a family therapist to the study of family dynamics in the nuclear age. He interviewed twenty Boston-area families with adolescent children, to discover how they communicate about the threat of nuclear war. These videotaped discussions suggest that many parents find the nuclear crisis overwhelming, and that many children, although feeling troubled themselves, are protecting their parents by not bringing up their worries, by saying that they aren't really bothered, or by trying to reassure their worried parents Parents' sense of helplessness and vulnerability in the face of the nuclear threat seemed to account for their difficulty in responding to their children's concerns. However, when parents shared the feelings and experiences they had during their own adolescence and young adulthood, at a time when nuclear fears were also high, it seemed to provide permission for their children to speak openly. The interviews revealed that adolescents respond positively when parents express clear viewpoints about specific aspects of the nuclear arms race, such as nuclear deterrence, or arms buildups, or when parents simply ask their children to share their ideas. Zeitlin found that in many of the interviews, the act of sharing concerns raised anxiety, especially in parents. However, this anxiety appeared to be linked with an increased sense of connectedness among family members.

Rudin has extended his clinical work with families to focus on the way in which parents address nuclear issues with their children. He recognized that many otherwise well-functioning parents have difficulty meeting the needs their children have as a result of the nuclear threat. In response, he designed one-session parenting groups to help parents evolve sound approaches to their children. These groups, conducted over a period of three years, have yielded valuable understanding about the functioning of families with regard to this issue. Parents expressed strong feelings of helplessness in dealing with their children around nuclear issues, and feared that family discussions would increase their children's burdens. Most of the parents were themselves nuclear-age children, and were deeply affected by their childhood experiences during the era of "duck and cover" drills, fall-out shelter frenzy, and brinksmanship situations like the 1962 Cuban missile crisis. They usually did not, and felt they should not, share their concerns with significant adults in their lives. The defenses they established in response to their fears seem to have shaped the way in which they dealt with nuclear concerns ever since, and seem also to influence the way in which they deal with their children around nuclear issues. Many parents used the setting of the parent groups to deal with their own fears as children, as well as their adult fears, for the first time. It seemed that this was a necessary step in enabling them to address their children's needs in an appropriate way.

Studies of young children: Focus on the extent of awareness of the nuclear threat in younger children (age 4-12) has so far been limited to studies that are almost entirely descriptive.

Friedman, 1983 (15). In an observational study of four-year-old pre-schoolers, Friedman sought to determine the extent to which children's play would reveal awareness about nuclear weapons. In a small-scale study, in which observation of play was made both before and after the presentation of children's stories involving conflict, and in which associative techniques were also used to elicit responses after the presentation, Friedman found that 12% of the children spontaneously included reference to nuclear weapons in their play and in their responses. Both teachers and parents of this group of young children were startled by the extent of the children's awareness.

Another source of information about younger children comes from videotaped interviews. Chivian and Snow's classroom discussions about nuclear issues with 1st, 3rd, 5th, 7th, and 9th grade students in the Boston area revealed knowledge and concern about nuclear weapons in each age group. (16) The responses of children in the different age groups also demonstrate how children at different developmental stages deal differently with their knowledge and their concern. Verdon-Roe's individual interviews with children from a wide range of ages and backgrounds also demonstrate a great deal of awareness and serious concern in the young. (17,18) While neither of these projects attempts to be representative, they begin to define a previously unexplored area, the effect on young children of growing up in an atmosphere of threat from nuclear weapons.

2. Studies conducted in Finland, Cananda, and Sweden and the Soviet Union, 1983-1984.

Finland - Solantaus et al., 1983 (19): This study was designed to determine how prevalent concern about war is among Finnish youth. The investigators were interested in this question in part because many adults held the opinion that in Finland, a country that is distant from the centers of world conflict, youth are not troubled by fear about war. The view was prevalent that young people are concerned only with their closest surroundings. The design of the study incorporated questions about war into a larger study project, "Juvenile Health Habit Study", to minimize bias that might affect a study dealing with only war and peace. A postal questionnaire was used for the representative sample of 6,851 young people, aged 12 to 18, who were drawn from the National Population Registry. The response rate was 81%. The questionnaire consisted of 108 items concerning demographic background, health habits, perceived health, and psychosomatic symptoms.

For the part of the study dealing with war and peace, the respondents' three main hopes and three main fears concerning their own life and future were asked in an open question. A subsample of 2,167 was given eight, additional, structured questions concerning discussion of peace and the threat of war, thinking about threat of war, nightmares or strong fear about war during preceding month, and attitudes about the possibility of helping prevent war through personal action. Results: Fear of war was the most frequently mentioned fear, with 81% of the entire group (77% of boys, 84% of girls) and almost 90% of the 12-year-olds, listing this as one of their three chief fears. Concern about work and employment was a distant second (40%). Finnish youth seem well informed about nuclear developments and the nature of nuclear war, and believe that even Finland could not escape its consequences. Girls were more likely than boys to experience strong anxiety and fear about war than boys (37% of girls, 15% of boys). While boys' anxiety dropped with age, for girls there was a slight increase. Girls were more likely than boys to discuss issues of war and peace with friends, and about one third of boys and girls discussed issues of war and peace at home.

Each of two variables, frequent thinking about war, and frequent discussions about war and peace with others, was positively correlated with optimism about the possibility of personally helping to prevent war, and optimism was positively correlated with school achievement. As for effect of socioeconomic class, those in the highest and lowest social classes thought most frequently about the threat of war. Belief that personal action could reduce this threat showed a similar distribution. In Finland, the authors conclude, low social class does not preclude concern with nation-wide and global issues.

Canada - Sommers, et al, 1983-1984 (20): This study sought to determine the impact on the emotional and psychological development of Canadian children and youth of living in the nuclear age. The research instrument embedded the nuclear issue among other subjects, on the model of Goldenring, to minimize bias. The study was carried out in three school boards of the city of Toronto, with different socioeconomic, ethnic and educational profiles, and assisted by the city's Medical Officer of Health. 1011 students from grades 6 through 13 participated.

Students were first asked to state their three strongest hopes and three greatest worries in an open-ended question. Then they were asked to rate the importance to them of 9 possible hopes and 9 possible worries ("things others your age hope for/worry about"), and asked to rate their importance (1 = least, 4 = most). Students were also asked to indicate the extent of personal concern and knowledge about, and personal influence over, three areas: unemployment rates, job and career plans, and the threat of nuclear war. Results: In answer to the question, "What three things do you worry about most?", war/peace was the first choice of 29%. More than half mentioned war/peace as one of their three concerns, slightly ahead of work/employment worries. On the list of nine worries, nuclear war ranked second-highest, with "my parents' death" being the only higher-ranked concern. As to frequency of thinking about nuclear war, 20% indicated once or twice weekly, and 10% indicated daily thoughts. Chief sources of information about nuclear issues were television (75%), newspapers and magazines (64%), teachers (39%), and families (31%). In contrast to the influence students felt they had over job and career plans, and even over employment conditions, 62% felt that they had no personal influence, and another 28% only a little personal influence in preventing nuclear attack, and viewed their parents as equally powerless. 50% felt, however, that the Canadian government could have a lot of influence in preventing nuclear war. When students were asked whether they or their families had taken some action to prevent nuclear war, 11% replied that they had, and 7% responded that their parents had.

As to the impact of the nuclear threat on plans for the future, most young people felt that their plans were not influenced at all, or only a little. Yet 28% reported that the nuclear threat had made them question "some" or "a lot" whether to marry and have children, and 24% felt that the nuclear threat leads them "somewhat" or "a lot" to live only for today.

This study showed a marked decrease with age in the proportion of students who mentioned war/peace as their first worry, from 37% in 7th graders, to 16% in 13th graders. The opposite trend existed with regard to work/employment (increase from 10% to 18%, in the same age span).

Sweden - Holmberg and Bergstroem, 1984 (21): This study aimed to determine how Swedish adolescents, aged 13-15, think and feel about the nuclear threat. 917 adolescents from 41 urban and rural schools, in different parts of Sweden, were surveyed. The Swedish Institute for Opinion Polls assisted the study, which was adapted from Goldenring and Doctor's design (see above). Concern about nuclear war was rated in comparison to 13 other worries known to affect Swedish teenagers. Participants were then asked to rank their top three of these 14 worries. After that, specific questions about nuclear war were asked.

Results: The number one worry, in mean score and in percent ranking was "nuclear war" (mean 3.20, where 1 = least, and 4 = most); 42% indicated that it was their greatest worry. The second highest rating (mean 2.58) was given to "parent dying". 11% ranked this first.

As to frequency of thinking about nuclear war, 24% of Swedish youth responded "weekly" or "daily". When asked if they thought nuclear war between the U.S. and U.S.S.R. was likely during their lifetime, 26% said, "probably" or "definitely", 47% weren't sure, and only 26% said "definitely not" or "probably not". Only 45% of Swedish teenagers said that a nuclear war could "probably" or "definitely" be prevented, while 23% said "probably not" and 9% "definitely not". 6% felt that they or their families would survive a nuclear war. More than 75% felt hopeful that nuclear war could be prevented through negotiations, a strong peace movement, many people protesting, and physicians working for prevention.

As for their perceptions of adults' attitudes, only 17% believed that adults are "very worried", while 46% thought that adults have very little concern, and 10% thought that adults are indifferent. 26% responded that they didn't know the attitude of adults at all. Teenagers' response to adults' apparent lack of concern is anger (30%), and fear (27%). They wonder why adults don't care (28%). The investigators refer to a significant discrepancy between children's perception of adult concern, and the extent of concern which adults express when they are surveyed. In adult surveys conducted in 1973 and 1982, 55% and 78%, respectively, considered nuclear war one of their three greatest worries. In a 1981 survey, 32% of adults also indicated that they think nuclear war will occur within ten years. Holmborg and Bergstroem conclude that "few adults appear to display their reaction to the nuclear threat by word or deed, despite their increasing fear."

63% of the youth in Holmborg and Bergstroem's study seldom or never talk to anyone about their nuclear fears. Those who do talk about them about them are most likely to share their concern with their peers, and of this subgroup, half also talk about their concerns with their parents. As for the role of the schools, 67% of respondents indicated that schools' teaching about nuclear issues is insufficient. There is a striking difference between the extent of worry expressed by girls and by boys: 67% of girls, but only 37% of boys are "very worried". Girls indicate higher level of worry on all 14 items in the list of worries.

Soviet Union - Chivian, Mack, Waletzky, et al., 1983 (22): In 1983, a study of the psychological effects of the threat of nuclear war on children of the Soviet Union was undertaken by a group of American investigators. Because of the unusual nature of this collaboration, it will be described in some detail. The project developed out of the cordial relationship between leading physicians from the Soviet Union and the United States, Dr. Evgeni Chazov, and Dr. Bernard Lown. These phsycians, motivated by the shared belief that physicians have the obligation to help prevent nuclear war, were co-founders of International Physicians for the Prevention of Nuclear War, which won the 1985 Nobel Peace Prize. With the assistance of Dr. Chazov, a team of five Americans, three of them psychiatrists, was able to conduct a study of Russian children that was similar to Chivian's American interview study and paralleled Goldenring and Doctor's American questionnaire study (see above). The goal was to determine Soviet adolescents' knowledge about, and attitude towards, nuclear weapons. The research was carried out at two summertime Pioneer Camps (Pioneers is a Soviet youth organization to which most children aged 10 to 15 belong). One camp, Gargarin, was for 350 children of familiies working at a domestic airport outside Moscow.

The other, Orlyenok, located on the Black Sea, was attended by 2,800 children from around the country selected for special achievement in academic work, in artistic endeavors, or in citizenship. The American research team was given free access to the two camps, followed their pre-determined research protocol, and used their own translator.

Interview study: Approximately 60 children, age 10 - 15, were selected, some by the American team, others by children's councils. Care was taken in the design of the interview process to avoid prior preparation or prompting. The American team was able to direct a skilled Soviet film crew, and retained full control over the nine hours of tape, which they later shortened into a representative 21 minute tape, after their return to the U.S.(23).

Questionnaire study: All the children for this part of the study attended the Orlyenok Camp. The Americans were able to select the camp sub-group to be questioned the evening before the study, with the children not informed of the subject matter beforehand. The age range was 9 to 17, with a mean age of 12.7. 60% were girls. In the first part of the questionnaire, children were asked to rank their degrees of worry about a variety of problems. In the second part, the following questions were asked.

1. Do you think a nuclear war between the U.S. and the U.S.S.R. will happen during your lifetime? 11.8%, yes; 54.5%, no; 33.7%, uncertain.

2. If there were a nuclear war, do you think that you and your family would survive? 2.9%, yes; 80.7%, no; 16.4%, uncertain.

3. If there were a nuclear war, do you think that the U.S. and the U.S.S.R. would survive it? 6.1%, yes; 78.9%, no; 15.0%, uncertain.

4. Do you think nuclear war between the U.S. and the U.S.S.R. can be prevented? 93.3%, yes; 2.8%, no; 3.9%, uncertain.

Both the interviews and the questionnaire results indicate that Soviet children are well informed about the dangers of nuclear weapons and are concerned about the possibility of nuclear war. They tend to believe that nuclear war is not survivable for them or for the countries engaged in it. As for the possibility of preventing nuclear war, they tend to feel optimistic. Their chief source of information about nuclear issues is television, though it appears that discussions about nuclear subjects often take place in both schools and homes.

Conclusions and discussion:

The first nuclear age studies of adolescents' expectations of war, undertaken in the United States in 1961, demonstrated substantial concern. When further attention was paid to this issue in 1977, more specific studies revealed that many American adolescents were aware of nuclear weapons and their effects, and that they were concerned that these weapons would be used in a nuclear war in their lifetime. The prevailing expectation among those studied was that neither they nor their families, nor probably even their country, would survive such a war. Feelings of powerlessness in influencing the future accompanied these fears. A number of recent studies have confirmed and elaborated the findings of the early descriptive studies of U.S. youth. These newer, increasingly quantitative studies have put adolescents' concern about nuclear war into a broad context, by comparing it with worry about other issues traditionally important to youth. The question has been raised by Coles (24) whether findings of widespread concern among adolescents apply to working class youths as well as to young people in the American middle class. The fact that a variety of questionnaire and interview studies, applied to large and diverse study samples, has yielded basically similar results strongly suggests that these concerns transcend class and ethnic lines.

Since 1983, studies of adolescents' attitudes have been undertaken in several other countries. Results are already available from the Soviet Union, Finland, Sweden, and Canada. The chief findings are that youth in each of these countries have considerable awareness about nuclear weapons, chiefly through mass media, and that worry about possible use of these weapons is widespread. While these are the predominant common findings, the studies also demonstrate significant differences in attitudes among the different nations' youth. Since the studies from the U.S., Canada, Sweden and the Soviet Union use similar research designs, based on the format of Goldenring and Doctor's American study, specific comparison of results is possible. As yet there is no research into attitudes of youth from developing nations.

In each country in which surveys included an open-ended question about young people's three greatest worries, nuclear war was included frequently, though there was a wide range among countries. (Table I)

Table I. Percentage of adolescents including nuclear war (or war)* as one of three chief worries.

United States (8)	12%
Canada (20)	51%
Finland (19)	80% (90% of 12 year-olds)

* In the U.S. study, 7% stated "nuclear war", 5% stated "war".

In the Finnish study, the percentages include both "nuclear war" and "war."

Large number of adolescents think often about the risk of nuclear war, and worry that it may, or believe that it will, take place in their lifetime. The high percentage of young people of different nations who think about nuclear war "often" or at least "weekly" is striking. A small but significant group of youth indicate that they think about the possibility of nuclear war daily (Table II). As many as 15% of U.S. youth and 32% of Swedish youth believe that nuclear war cannot be prevented. American adolescents consider it most likely, and also most survivable, while Soviet youth consider it least likely and least survivable. Even though young people tend to be fearful that nuclear war will happen, most feel that it is preventable, with Soviet youth considering prevention most likely, and Swedish youth, least likely. It would be interesting to have more information on these reported areas of contrast, and on their genesis.

Table II. Frequency of thinking about nuclear war (or war+)

	often #	weekly @	daily
United States (8)	33%		
(12)		25%	11%
(9)	30%(1982)		
	7%(1985		
Canada (20)		20%	10%
Sweden		24% weekly or daily	
Finland		28%	8%

+ the wording in the Finnish study was "war"

"often" was the wording used in two American studies (2) (9)

@ "weekly" and "daily" was the wording used in one study (11), and in the Canadian, Swedish, and Finnish studies.

Table III. Comparison of American, Swedish and Soviet adolescents' attitudes about likelihood of nuclear war, survivability, and the possibility of prevention.*

		American	Swedish	Soviet
1. Do you think a nuclear war between the U.S. and the U.S.S.R. will happen during your lifetime?	yes + no # uncertain	38.5% 16 44.5	26% 26 48	11.8% 54.5 33.7
2. If there were a nuclear war, do you think you and your family would survive?	yes no uncertain	16.5% 41.5% 41.1	6% 68 26	2.9% 80.7 16.4
3. If there were a nuclear war, do you think that the U.S. and the U.S.S.R. would survive it? @	yes no uncertain	22% 38 39.5	13% 64 23	6.1% 78.9 15
4. Do you think nuclear war between the U.S. and the U.S.S.R. can be prevented?	yes no uncertain	65% 14.5% 20	45% 32 23	93.3% 2.8 3.9

* Data used with permission, Dr. Eric Chivian (22)

+ Yes = definitely or probably yes

no = definitely or probably no

@ American children were asked only about survival of the U.S.

Although a majority of adolescents state that their future plans have not been affected by the nuclear threat, substantial numbers of U.S. and Canadian youth state that it affects their plans for marriage and having children. Many young people indicate that the nuclear threat to their future fosters in them an attitude of living only for today. (U.S., 24%; Canada, 9% influences "a lot", 15%, "some".)

Whether these stated expectations and perceptions correspond to actual effects of the nuclear threat on future choices, or on present life styles, is unknown. Perhaps long-term studies will yield some answers. The groups of young people most preoccupied with the nuclear threat, those most pessimistic, and those who state that their future plans are being affected by the nuclear threat, warrant special focus. We need to learn not only why these young people are affected particularly strongly, we also need to determine whether their perception of the nuclear threat heightens their vulnerability to other stresses.

Students in some countries indicated that they could personally contribute to the prevention of war (Finland, Soviet Union), or that groups of individuals working together could make a difference (Sweden), while most Canadian students felt that there was little that they or their parents could do. In response to a question about efforts to diminish the nuclear danger (U.S., Canada), few young people indicated that either they or their parents had undertaken any personal action.

Most young people in the countries studied rarely discuss their nuclear fears with others, and very few ever discuss them with their parents (Table IV).

Table IV. Frequency of talking with parents about nuclear war (or war+) concerns.

	not at all	rarely
United States (8)	51%	39%
Finland (19)	70%	
Sweden (21)	63% seldom or never	

+ in the Finnish study, the wording was "war"

As a result of the family avoidance of nuclear issues, children may know little about their parents' attitudes and may interpret adult silence as lack of concern, which leaves them puzzled, angry, and afraid (Sweden). Beginning studies of the family dynamics that evolve in response to the nuclear threat indicate that parents tend to feel helpless in the face of the nuclear threat and seem not to know how to meet their children's needs. When parents in effect offer their children neither support nor guidance, inadequate coping in the face of the nuclear threat may be transmitted from one generation to another. In families who do not address nuclear realities, even though they may be well aware of the threat these pose for family continuity, family members are left without each other's support in the face of a difficult problem, and are also deprived of the possibility for concerted action to address the danger. Findings suggest that many parents may need help in evolving sound approaches to their children with regard to nuclear issues. Parents can help each other develop the necessary new skills (25) and health professionals and educators have the opportunity, and the professional responsibility, to apply their experience to the problem of parenting in the nuclear age (26, 27).

As to the extent of awareness and concern about nuclear issues at different ages, very little research has been carried out with children younger than 11 or 12, and those studies that exist are mainly descriptive. They indicate that children, down to the early elementary school years, are often spared neither awareness nor concern, and that even some pre-schoolers express nuclear awareness in their play, often to the surprise of parents and teachers. That there are few studies of young children seems related not only to the newness of the field of nuclear psychology. Impressions that the young suffer little effect may be one factor. Another may be the concern that studying children's knowledge and feelings about nuclear realities may induce anxiety, a point which Alvik begins to address (28). Research about the nuclear threat and its impact tends to be psychologically difficult for researchers exploring any age group, because of the painful realities it addresses (29). This may be especially true in considering effects on young children. Engel focuses on nonintrusive and supportive ways in which adults can learn about possible nuclear concerns in young children (30).

Several studies demonstrate a large shift with age in concern about nuclear war. The youngest children inc uded in the quantitative studies (usually 11 to 12 year-olds) worried about the possibility of nuclear war considerably more often, or ranked and rated it considerably higher among their worries, than did older students, with the trend of decreasing concern with increasing age persisting through the college years. In the American study that included college students, this group thought about nuclear war markedly less often, and considered nuclear war less likely, than any other age group, younger or older (Table V).

Table V. Shifts with age in thinking and worrying about nuclear war (war+)

Finland (19)
(listing war
as first worry)

11	12	13	14	15	16	17	18	19	19-22	over 22
	79%		72%		57%		48%			

Canada 20)
(listing nuclear
war as first worry)

11	12	13	14	15	16	17	18	19	19-22	over 22
	37%		20%	24%			26%	16%		

United States
(mean worry rating
of nuclear war,
1 = not w.,
4 = very w. (8))

11	12	13	14	15	16	17	18	19	19-22	over 22
	3.01			2.73			2.00			

(thinking about nuclear
war daily (12)

11	12	13	14	15	16	17	18	19	19-22	over 22
			15%				5%			16%

+ in the Finnish study, the wording was "war".

This age shift merits consideration. Is the high level of concern in those at the youngest end of this range a sensitive barometer of fear in the world they perceive, untempered by defenses that develop at a later stage? In turn, among college students, is the relatively infrequent thinking about, and low concern about, nuclear dangers in part a measure of the difficulty in simultaneously planning for the future, and contemplating the nuclear threat to that future?

A deeper understanding of the developmental effects on perception of the nuclear threat is needed and will be helpful in interpreting age differences. In turn, the psychological impact of the nuclear threat on development needs detailed, long-term study. Escalona and Lifton have discussed developmental aspects of growing up in the nuclear age from a theoretical point of view (31, 32).

As for sex differences in concern about nuclear war or war in general, the Swedish and Finnish studies demonstrate marked differences, with girls indicating substantially greater concern than boys (Table VI). Solantaus et al. (18) speculate that the difference in boys' and girls' attitudes towards war and aggression in general, and the different role that men and women have played in past wars, may be factors in this striking contrast. If boys' upbringing and conditioning desensitizes them to negative aspects of war, this is particularly important in the nuclear age, and has ramifications for both parenting and teaching.

Table VI. Differences in boys' and girls' worry about war+ or nuclear war.

	Boys	Girls
Finland: strong anxiety or fear (19)	15%	37%
Sweden: very worried:(21)	37%	67%

+ Finnish wording.

In the studies of adolescents from the four countries in which data permitted such analysis, there was a positive correlation between frequent worry about nuclear war (or "war", in the Finnish study), high achievement in school, history of discussing nuclear concerns with others, and optimism that nuclear war could be prevented (United States, Canada, Sweden, Finland). The data from the Soviet Union did not lend itself to this analysis, but since optimism among Soviet youth was high, and the sample was drawn from a camp for highly achieving students, a similar relationship may exist. Awareness of nuclear realities leads to concern in thoughtful adolescents. The question of whether greater awareness results from family discussion, or whether young people's thoughtful awareness about nuclear issues results in their raising the subject at home more readily, cannot be answered from the available data. Both may be true. A likely explanation for the correlation of frequent worry, sharing, and optimism is that thinking about the nuclear threat, coupled with support from others, is a prerequisite for contemplating and searching for solutions to the nuclear dilemma.

It is not possible to prevent young people's nuclear awareness. The danger posed by nuclear weapons is real.

Therefore it is appropriate and adaptive that it be recognized. The young will be least harmed by the nuclear reality, about which they usually first learn from the mass media, if caretaking adults are willing to address these issues with them, in a thoughtful and age-appropriate way, taking into account their developmental stage, their vulnerabilities and their need to know. What can be and needs to be prevented is the hopelessness that may result when young people's awareness is unaccompanied by support, when their legitimate concern fails to be validated, or when their perception that adults are failing to address nuclear problems remains unchallenged by meaningful action. These conditions that feed young people's hopelessness need to be vigorously addressed. It is a task for families and for schools.

Studies indicate that many high school students, though aware of and concerned about nuclear weapons, are poorly informed about basic aspects of the nuclear arms race (33,34). Many are aware that they are poorly informed, and express the need for more information (3, 21, 35). Sound approaches for helping the young in schools include several crucial elements. Adolescents and children need a supportive environment for raising their concerns and questions. Teaching needs to be age-appropriate, and designed not to overwhelm students with anxiety about a terrifying subject. Mental health professionals can assist educators in evolving teaching approaches that take these factors into consideration (27). Students need to learn that the nuclear situation is complex and that there are diverse views about ways to create a safer world. The goal should be to teach them to think critically, and to form their own opinions. Most significantly, they need to learn about the power of individuals to influence the world around them, by being encouraged to address problems that affect their communities. If they discover that they are able to help bring about needed changes, they can begin to imagine the possibility of influencing larger, more complex problems in their world.

Various curriculum approaches based on these premises have been developed in the United States by scientists, teachers, and others concerned about the nuclear crisis, and the well-being of children in the face of it (36, 37, 38, 39, 40). Such education represents many challenges. Markusen discusses motivations for educating students to recognize and deal with today's nuclear danger (41). He refers to youth education in Germany before and during World War II, education that increased acceptance of genocide, and he argues that the lesson to be learned is that education in the nuclear age must avoid increasing the likelihood of nuclear holocaust. Instead, education needs to play a role in diminishing the threat of nuclear war by producing a generation that is equipped to address this problem. A U.S. government primer for kindergarten through high school field-tested in schools in 26 states (42), which advocates shelter preparation as a solution for the event of nuclear war, but teaches nothing about the need to prevent such war, appears disturbingly inadequate from this point of view.

Tizard addresses the fact that as yet little is understood about the interaction of knowledge, anxiety and attitudes in children, and that we do not yet know what constitutes the best educational approach in the nuclear age (43). Studies are needed to determine the effects of different approaches. A beginning has been made. Snow has gathered data about high school students' responses to an extended curriculum dealing with the nuclear arms race (35), and London has measured short-term impact of a day-long nuclear education project for high school students (44). No study of long-term effects of any nuclear education program has yet been undertaken.

The study of the effect of the nuclear threat on children and adolescents is a field which has developed rapidly in the last few years, after an early start in 1961. There remain many significant questions about young people's attitudes in this realm, about the forces shaping them, and about the effect which the nuclear threat has on their psychological development. How young people develop and cope with these problems is likely to play a great role in the fate of mankind.

REFERENCES

1. Swedish Institute for Opinion Polls, 1973, 1981, 1982.

2. Kramer, B.M., Kalick, S.M., Milburn, M.A. Attitudes towards nuclear weapons and nuclear war: 1945 - 1982. Journal of Social Issues 1983: 39: 501-530.

3. Yankelovich, D., Doble, J. The public mood: nuclear weapons and the U.S.S.R. Foreign Affairs 1984: 63, #1, 33 - 46.

4. Schwebel, M. Nuclear cold war: student opinion and professional responsibility. In: Schwebel, M. ed. Behavioral science and human survival. Palo Alto, Calif.: Bahavioral Sciences Press, 1965.

5. Escalona, S.K. Children and the threat of nuclear war. In: Schwebel, M., ed. Behavioral science and human survival. Palo Alto, Calif.: Behavioral Sciences Press, 1965.

6. Beardslee, W.R., Mack, J.E. The impact on children and adolescents of nuclear developments. In: Rogers, R., ed. Psychosocial aspects of nuclear developments, Task Force Report #20. Washington, D.C.: American Psychiatric Association, 1982.

7. Goodman, L.A., Mack, J.E., Beardslee, W.R., Snow, R.M. The threat of nuclear war and the nuclear arms race: adolescent experience and perceptions. Political Psychology 1983: #4 (3): 501-530.

8. Goldenring, J.M., Doctor, R. California adolescents' concern about the threat of nuclear war. Presented at Fourth Congress of International Physicians for the Prevention of Nuclear War (IPPNW), Helsinki, Finland, June 1984.

9. Bachman, J.G. American high school seniors view the military: 1976 - 1982. Armed Forces and Soceity 1983: 10, #1, 86-104.

10. Bachman, J.G. Personal communication with Monika Eisenbud, 1985.

11. Gould, J.B., Berger Gould, B., Eden, E. The threat of war in the minds of junior high school students in the U.S.A. Presented at symposium: The psychological effect of the nuclear threat on children: strategies for action. University of California, Berkeley, California, December 1984.

12. Van Hoorn, J., French, P. Perception and reaction to the threat of nuclear war: a life-span perspective. Presented at symposium: the psychological effect of the nuclear threat on children: strategies for action. University of California, Berkeley, California, December, 1984.

13. Zeitlin, S. What do we tell mom and dad? The Family Therapy Networker 1984: 8, #2: 31ff.

14. Rudin, E. Written communication.

15. Friedman, B. Preschoolers' awareness of the nuclear threat. California Association for the Education of Young Children Newsletter 1984: 12: 2.

16. Chivian, E., Snow, R.M. There's a nuclear war going on inside me: What children are saying about nuclear war. Videotape of classroom discussions. Boston, Massachusetts: IPPNW, 1983.

17. Verdon-Roe, V., Thierman, E., Thierman, I. In the nuclear shadow: what can children tell us? Videotapes of children's interview responses. Santa Cruz, California: Educational Film and Video Project, 1983.

18. Verdon-Roe, V. Growing up in the nuclear age: What the children can tell us. East West Journal 1983: January: 24-31.

19. Solantaus, T., Rimpela, M., Taipale, V. The threat of war in the minds of 12 - 18 year-olds in Finland. Lancet 1984: 1: 784-785.

20. Sommers, F., Goldberg, S., Levinson,, D., Ross, C., LaCombe, S. Children's mental health and the threat of nuclear war: a Canadian pilot study. Presented at Fourth Congress of IPPNW, Helsinki, Finland, June 1984.

21. Holmborg, P.O., Bergstroem, A. A survey of attitudes of Swedish adolescents towards nuclear war. Presented at Fourth Congress of IPPNW, Helsinki, Finalnd, June 1984.

22. Chivian, E., Mack, J.E., Waletzky, J., Lazaroff, C., Doctor, R., Goldenring, J.M. Soviet children and the threat of nuclear war. American Journal of Orthopsychiatry 1985 (Accepted for publication).

23. Chivian, E., Mack, J.E., Waletzky, J. What Soviet children are saying about nuclear weapons. Videotape of interviews with 10 - 15 year-olds in the Soviet Union. Boston, Massachusetts: IPPNW, 1984.

24. Coles, R. The doomsayers. Class politics and the nuclear freeze: the numbing polemics of Dr. Caldicott. Boston Observer 1984: 3, #10 1ff.

25. Cloud, K., Deegan, E., Evans, A, Iman, H., Singer, B. Watermelons, not war! A support book for parenting in the nuclear age. Philadelphia, Pennsylvania: New Society Publishers, 1984.

26. Schwebel, M. Effects of the nuclear war threat on children and teenagers: implications for professionals. American Journal of Orthopsychiatry 1982. 52: 608-618.

27. Eisenbud, M.M. Consulting to schools in the nuclear age: an evolving role for mental health professionals. Presented at symposium: Child Psychiatry in the Nuclear Age. Thirty-first Annual Meeting of the American Academy of Child Psychiatry, Toronto, Canada, October, 1984.

28. Alvik, T. The problem of anxiety in connection with investigations concerning children's conception of war and peace. Scandinavian Journal of Educational Research 1968: 215-233.

29. Beardslee, W.R., Mack, J.E. Adolescents and the threat of nuclear war: the evolution of a perspective. Yale Journal of Biology and Medicine 1983; 56: 79-91.

30. Engel, B. Between feeling and fact: listening to children. In: A special issue: Education and the threat of nuclear war. Harvard Educational Review 1984; 54, #3: 282-303.

31. Escalona, S. Growing up with the threat of nuclear war: some indirect effects on personality development. American Journal of Orthopsychiatry 1982; 52: 600-607.

32. Lifton, R.J. Implications of the arms race upon children. Presented before U.S. House of Representatives Select Committee on Children, Youth and Families. Washington, D.C.: U.S. Congressional Report, September 20, 1983.

33. Zweigenhaft, R.L. The psychological effect of living in a nuclear age. Unpublished manuscript, 1983.

34. French, P. Ignorance and the capacity to countenance nuclear war. Unpublished manuscript, 1983.

35. Snow, R.M. Responses of adolescents to a course about the nuclear arms race. Written communication, 1984.

36. Alexander, S., ed. Educators for Social Responsibility Bibliography of Nuclear Education Resources. Cambridge, Massachusetts: Educators for Social Responsibility, 1984.

37. Snow, R.M., Austill, C., Bowditch, B., et al. Decision making in a nuclear age. Curriculum for high school students. Weston, Massachusetts: Halcyon House, 1983.

38. Union of Concerned Scientists and the National Education Association. Choices: a unit on conflict and nuclear war. Curriculum for junior high school students. Washington, D.C.: National Education Association, 1983.

39. Berman, S. Perspectives: a teaching guide to concepts of peace. Curriculum for kindergarten through high school. Cambridge, Massachusetts: Educators for Social Responsibility, 1984.

40. Berman, S. The participation series. Social studies, science and mathematics curriculum projects. Cambridge, Massachusetts: Educators for Social Responsibility, 1984.

41. Markusen, E., Harris, J.B. The role of education in preventing nuclear war. In: A special issue:

education and the threat of nuclear war. Harvard Education Review 1984; 54, #3: 282-303.

42. Federal Emergency Management Agency. Emergency Management Instruction Curriculum and Teachers' Resource Manual. Curriculum for grades K - 12. Draft 1G. Washington, D.C.: U.S. Government Printing Office, 1981.

43. Tizard, B. Problematic aspects of nuclear education. In: A special issue: education and the threat of nuclear war. Harvard Education Review 1984; 54, #3: 271-181.

44. London, D. Anxiety and attitudes in high school students before and after an educational workshop on nuclear war issues. Unpublished manuscript, 1985.

NOTES ON CONTRIBUTORS

ELLEN BECKER, M.F.C.C., is a psychotherapist in private practice in Oakland, California. She is a founding member of Psychotherapists for Social Responsibility, a member of Interhelp, and author of "The Nuclear Threat and the Therapeutic Process", in <u>Therapy Now</u> Magazine, Summer, 1984.

BENINA BERGER GOULD, L.C.S.W., is a family therapist in private practice in Berkeley, California. She is the Project Director of the Nuclear Ecology Research Project, a project of Peace and Common Security, where she is a Fellow. She is Chairperson of the American Family Therapy Association Task Force on Family Systems and the Nuclear Issue, and has published a number of articles in this field. Benina has twice been co-leader of the Association for Humanistic Psychology delegation to the U.S.S.R.

EVE EDEN, L.C.S.W., works with Social Advocates for Youth, a youth service agency in Cupertino, California, and has a private practice in Santa Cruz. She works with a broad range of adolescents -- from the sons and daughters of Lockheed employees in Sunnyvale, California, to the generally progressive teenagers of Santa Cruz, dealing with the issue of nuclear war in clinical as well as educational settings.

MONIKA EISENBUD, M.D., is Clinical Instructor in Psychiatry at Harvard Medical School, and has a private practice in Newton, Massachusetts. She is Vice Chair of the American Academy on Clinical and Developmental

Aspects of the Nuclear Threat, and is a frequent speaker for Physicians for Social Responsibility.

JEFFREY GOULD, M.D., pediatrician and neonatologist, is Associate Professor of Maternal and Child Health at the School of Public Health, University of California at Berkeley. He is Research Director of the Nuclear Ecology Research Project, and a Fellow of Peace and Common Security.

BARBARA GREEN, L.C.S.W., is a psychotherapist in private practice in Berkeley, California. She is on the National Council of Interhelp, and is a member of Psychotherapists for Social Responsibility.

HOWARD HAMBURGER, M.F.C.C., is a psychotherapist in private practice in Berkeley and Fremont, California. He is a founding member of Psychotherapists for Social Responsibility, a member of the National Council of Interhelp and the author of "Joy and Empowerment," in the Winter, 1986, issue of <u>Awakening in the Nuclear Age Journal</u>.

RON LALLY, Ed.D. is the Director of the Center for Child and Family Studies at the Far West Laboaratory for Educational Research and Development. He has written extensively on child-rearing in relation to social issues, and is currently finishing a book called, <u>Raising Young Children While Working</u>. He is active with Beyond War and CEASE, and is one of the creators of the International Association for the Study of Children in the Nuclear Age.

JOYCE LASHOF, M.D., is the Dean of the School of Public Health at the University of California at Berkeley. She has written extensively on the subject of health policy, and is a member of Physicians for Social Responsibility.

JOHN E. MACK, M.D., is Professor of Psychiatry at the Cambridge Hospital, Harvard Medical School. His professional focus is on the application of psychological insights to biography and to social and political problems in the nuclear age, and he has written widely in this field. He is a member of Physicians for Social Responsibility and an active participant in International Physicians for the Prevention of Nuclear War.

ALAN MARCUS, of Carmel, California, is a writer, the author of numerous novels and screen plays. He is the founder of the Monterey Coalition for a Nuclear Freeze, and has been a peace activist ever since the night thirty-five years ago when he and his infant daughter were awakened, in their home in Southern California, by the bright reflection of an atom bomb test in Nevada.

LOTTE MARCUS, Ph.D., is currently Staff Psychologist for Cross-Cultrual Medicine at Natividad Medical Center in Salinas, and is also in private practice. She is a member of Physicians for Social Responsibility, and has had a long and active career in peace work, with a particular interest in peace education.

SUSAN MOON is a writer, editor, and the publisher of Open Books, in Berkeley, California, which focuses on publishing books about the peace movement. She is a member of Parenting in the Nuclear Age, and is one of the editors and authors of that group's booklet for parents, What Shall We Tell the Children?. She is co-author and editor, with Jackie Cabasso, of Risking Peace: Why We Sat in the Road, a chronicle of nonviolent protest at the Livermore National Weapons Laboratory. She has two teenage sons.

LAURIE OLSEN, M.A.T., works in the field of youth policy and advocacy. She is Executive Director of the Citizens' Policy Center, a non-profit youth organization in Oakland, California. She was the architect and Director of the Nuclear Action for Youth Project and the Youth Peace Fund, and she co-authored Our Future at Stake: A Teenager's Guide to the Arms Race, as well as numerous other publications about the needs and concerns of youth. She is a former high school history teacher, and now the mother of two children.

WENDY ROBERTS, M.S.W., works as a counselor and consultant in planning strategies for personal, social and organizational transformation. She was founder and director of The Day Before project, which organized community forums, nationwide, on public responses to the nuclear threat, particularly in relation to the television film, The Day After.

RICHARD SMOKE, Ph.D., is Research Director of the center for Foreign Policy Development and Professor of Political Science, both at Brown University. He is cofounder and former Executive Director of Peace and Common Security, a non-profit foundation for the study of peaceful alternatives to the arms race, and is presently a member of the the Board. He has published widely in the field of international security policy.

TYTTI SOLANTAUS, M.D., is Child Psychiatrist at the Department of Public Health Science, University of Helsinki, Finland. She is active with Internatioanl Physicians for the Prevention of Nuclear War, and an editor of the IPPNW publication, The Impact of the Threat of Nuclear War on Children and Adolescents.

JUDITH VAN HOORN, Ph.D., is Assistant Professor at the University of the Pacific, in Stockton, California, in the field of early childhood education. She has been conducting research on adolescents' and adults' attitudes toward nuclear weapons and war since 1983. She is the author of numerous papers and presentations on young people and the arms race, and she works actively with Beyond War, in Stockton.

DEBORAH WEINSTEIN, M.F.C.C., is a psychotherapist in private practice in San Francisco. She is one of the cofounders of Waking Up in the Nuclear Age, is a member of both Psychotherapists for Social Responsibility and Interhelp, and has led "Despair and Empowerment" workshops since 1981. She recently returned from her first trip to the Soviet Union.